International Adoptions

Other Books of Related Interest:

Opposing Viewpoints Series
Celebrity Culture

At Issue Series
Do Children Have Rights?

Current Controversies Series
Aid to Africa

"Congress shall make
no law . . . abridging
the freedom of speech,
or of the press."

First Amendment to the U.S. Constitution

The basic foundation of our democracy is the First Amendment guarantee of freedom of expression. The Opposing Viewpoints Series is dedicated to the concept of this basic freedom and the idea that it is more important to practice it than to enshrine it.

OPPOSING VIEWPOINTS® SERIES

International Adoptions

Margaret Haerens, book editor

GREENHAVEN PRESS
A part of Gale, Cengage Learning

GALE
CENGAGE Learning™

Detroit • New York • San Francisco • New Haven, Conn • Waterville, Maine • London

GALE
CENGAGE Learning™

Christine Nasso, *Publisher*
Elizabeth Des Chenes, *Managing Editor*

© 2011 Greenhaven Press, a part of Gale, Cengage Learning.

Gale and Greenhaven Press are registered trademarks used herein under license.

For more information, contact:
Greenhaven Press
27500 Drake Rd.
Farmington Hills, MI 48331-3535
Or you can visit our Internet site at gale.cengage.com

Articles in Greenhaven Press anthologies are often edited for length to meet page requirements. In addition, original titles of these works are changed to clearly present the main thesis and to explicitly indicate the author's opinion. Every effort is made to ensure that Greenhaven Press accurately reflects the original intent of the authors. Every effort has been made to trace the owners of copyrighted material.

Cover Image copyright © iStockPhoto.com/Vetta Collection.

LIBRARY OF CONGRESS CATALOGING-IN-PUBLICATION DATA

International adoptions / Margaret Haerens, book editor.
    p. cm. -- (Opposing viewpoints)
    Includes bibliographical references and index.
    ISBN 978-0-7377-4970-0 (hardcover) -- ISBN 978-0-7377-4971-7 (pbk.)
    1. Intercountry adoption--United States--Juvenile literature. 2. Interracial adoption--United States--Juvenile literature. 3. Intercountry adoption--Juvenile literature. 4. Interracial adoption--Juvenile literature. I. Haerens, Margaret.
    HV875.5.I5735 2010
    362.734--dc22
                                     2010011351

Printed in the United States of America
1 2 3 4 5 6 7 14 13 12 11 10

Contents

Chapter 3: What Are the Consequences of International Adoptions?

Chapter 4: What Changes Should Be Made to the International Adoption Process?

Why Consider Opposing Viewpoints?

"The only way in which a human being can make some approach to knowing the whole of a subject is by hearing what can be said about it by persons of every variety of opinion and studying all modes in which it can be looked at by every character of mind. No wise man ever acquired his wisdom in any mode but this."

John Stuart Mill

In our media-intensive culture it is not difficult to find differing opinions. Thousands of newspapers and magazines and dozens of radio and television talk shows resound with differing points of view. The difficulty lies in deciding which opinion to agree with and which "experts" seem the most credible. The more inundated we become with differing opinions and claims, the more essential it is to hone critical reading and thinking skills to evaluate these ideas. Opposing Viewpoints books address this problem directly by presenting stimulating debates that can be used to enhance and teach these skills. The varied opinions contained in each book examine many different aspects of a single issue. While examining these conveniently edited opposing views, readers can develop critical thinking skills such as the ability to compare and contrast authors' credibility, facts, argumentation styles, use of persuasive techniques, and other stylistic tools. In short, the Opposing Viewpoints Series is an ideal way to attain the higher-level thinking and reading skills so essential in a culture of diverse and contradictory opinions.

In addition to providing a tool for critical thinking, Opposing Viewpoints books challenge readers to question their own strongly held opinions and assumptions. Most people form their opinions on the basis of upbringing, peer pressure, and personal, cultural, or professional bias. By reading carefully balanced opposing views, readers must directly confront new ideas as well as the opinions of those with whom they disagree. This is not to simplistically argue that everyone who reads opposing views will—or should—change his or her opinion. Instead, the series enhances readers' understanding of their own views by encouraging confrontation with opposing ideas. Careful examination of others' views can lead to the readers' understanding of the logical inconsistencies in their own opinions, perspective on why they hold an opinion, and the consideration of the possibility that their opinion requires further evaluation.

Evaluating Other Opinions

To ensure that this type of examination occurs, Opposing Viewpoints books present all types of opinions. Prominent spokespeople on different sides of each issue as well as well-known professionals from many disciplines challenge the reader. An additional goal of the series is to provide a forum for other, less known, or even unpopular viewpoints. The opinion of an ordinary person who has had to make the decision to cut off life support from a terminally ill relative, for example, may be just as valuable and provide just as much insight as a medical ethicist's professional opinion. The editors have two additional purposes in including these less known views. One, the editors encourage readers to respect others' opinions—even when not enhanced by professional credibility. It is only by reading or listening to and objectively evaluating others' ideas that one can determine whether they are worthy of consideration. Two, the inclusion of such viewpoints encourages the important critical thinking skill of objectively evaluating an author's credentials and bias. This evaluation will illuminate an author's reasons for taking a particular stance on an issue and will aid in readers' evaluation of the author's ideas.

It is our hope that these books will give readers a deeper understanding of the issues debated and an appreciation of the complexity of even seemingly simple issues when good and honest people disagree. This awareness is particularly important in a democratic society such as ours in which people enter into public debate to determine the common good. Those with whom one disagrees should not be regarded as enemies but rather as people whose views deserve careful examination and may shed light on one's own.

Thomas Jefferson once said that "difference of opinion leads to inquiry, and inquiry to truth." Jefferson, a broadly educated man, argued that "if a nation expects to be ignorant and free . . . it expects what never was and never will be." As individuals and as a nation, it is imperative that we consider the opinions of others and examine them with skill and discernment. The Opposing Viewpoints Series is intended to help readers achieve this goal.

David L. Bender and Bruno Leone,
Founders

Introduction

On January 12, 2010, a 7.0 magnitude earthquake hit the small country of Haiti in the Caribbean. The epicenter of the quake was approximately sixteen miles west of the capital city, Port-au-Prince, a densely packed metropolis of more than 3 million people—many of them living in poorly constructed slums in the hillsides on the outskirts of the capital. The devastating power of the earthquake and its subsequent aftershocks demolished buildings, causing the collapse of homes, jails, retail shops, government offices, hospitals—in many cases, entire city blocks. Thousands of people were killed instantly as buildings fell on top of them; others were trapped by debris and hoped to be saved. Many of them were. Others were not so lucky. On February 10, 2010, the Haitian government estimated that approximately 230,000 people were killed by the earthquake, and 300,000 had been injured.

Like in the Indonesian tsunami in 2004, the Haitian earthquake tore apart families, resulting in thousands of children orphaned or separated from their parents. In many cases, parents were killed and children survived. With the Haitian government pretty much immobilized—government buildings had collapsed and government records were destroyed—chaos and panic began to spread across the country as nongovernmental organizations and international organizations such as the United Nations scrambled to help the children that had been orphaned, abandoned, or separated from their parents. Fears that these children would starve or go without medical care were very real.

As heartbreaking videos of the suffering Haitian people were broadcast worldwide, foreign governments, charitable organizations, and even motivated individuals began to mobilize to help. The U.S. government pressured the beleaguered Haitian government to rush adoptions that were in the pipeline to their conclusion. In these cases, the paperwork was already complete and the requests were quickly granted; dozens of Haitian children were flown from Haiti and reunited with their relieved adoptive parents in the United States.

Many children, however, were not so lucky. They remained in orphanages or on the street, some of them hurt and others needing food and medical care. In light of little government help or oversight, groups—both sanctioned and unsanctioned—attempted to step in and help in any way they could. The situation had the potential for disaster.

On January 29, 2010, ten American missionaries were arrested on a bus near the border of the Dominican Republic when they were found with thirty-three Haitian orphans. Haitian officials accused the Americans of taking the children without the proper paperwork, eventually charging them with kidnapping. It was revealed that several of the children were not orphans—they had surviving parents. Officials claimed that the missionaries lied to anguished and desperate parents so they could take the children across the border. The American missionaries claimed that they did not mean to break any laws; they were only concerned with getting the children to safety at another orphanage run by the missionary group in the Dominican Republican, where the children would be provided with food, safe shelter, and ample medical care.

The case of the American missionaries reflects the crux of the debate over the issue of international adoption. When people see a child in peril or suffering, their first impulse is to take that child from that situation and provide him or her with a safe place. They see the matter as one of compassion—as when a family seeks to adopt a child who needs a permanent, loving home. Yet critics argue that children cannot be ripped away from their local communities without established and well-considered protocols and a thorough legal review to protect them. Without strong regulations and a well-ordered adoption system, children can be vulnerable to a range of dangerous and unsavory characters who are looking to exploit and abuse them. In the aftermath of the Indonesian tsunami, fears spread that pedophiles and child traffickers were kidnapping children. Although these situations are actually quite rare, the threat is very real—and governments have a responsibility to protect the most vulnerable, especially in the aftermath of traumatic and catastrophic natural disasters, such as the tsunami and the earthquake.

The tension between the governmental obligations to protect children and the human desire to help orphaned and abandoned kids by finding them permanent homes is a source of ongoing debate over international adoption. The authors of the viewpoints presented in *Opposing Viewpoints: International Adoptions* discuss many of these issues in the following chapters: Should International Adoptions Be Encouraged? How Do Celebrity Adoptions Affect the Debate over International Adoptions? What Are the Consequences of International Adoptions? and What Changes Should Be Made to the International Adoption Process? This volume examines the controversy over international adoption, the different approaches to dealing with children who have been orphaned or abandoned, and ways to adjust the process of adoption to facilitate a smoother transition for adoptive families and adopted children.

OPPOSING
VIEWPOINTS®
SERIES

CHAPTER 1

Should International Adoptions Be Encouraged?

Chapter Preface

The practice of international adoption has come under fire in recent years. Whereas once it was considered a worthy solution to the worldwide problem of orphans and abandoned children, critics of international adoption argue that it is not the best option for these children. They argue that a better solution is to keep them within their own country and connected to their native culture. This raging debate has certainly taken a toll on the practice of international adoption. The numbers tell the story: In 2004, the number of foreign children adopted by U.S families was 22,990; in 2009, the number had dropped to 12,753.

This precipitous drop in international adoptions can be attributed to a few key factors. The number of countries allowing international adoptions has decreased significantly, and countries that do allow it have passed draconian regulations that make it very difficult for foreign-born parents to come in and adopt children. Many of these countries have been appalled by and have reacted to the reported abuses in international adoptions, which include cases of child trafficking, baby buying, fraud, kidnapping, and sexual exploitation of children. Such horrific abuses, although relatively rare, have resulted in much tighter adoption laws—or even have prompted countries to completely shut down international adoptions altogether.

Many countries that are against international adoptions argue that it is not in the best interest of the children to separate them from their cultural heritage. At all costs, they assert, orphaned or abandoned children should be kept within their country of origin. They institute restrictions that require children to be held for long periods in orphanages while they explore in-country options. Several of these countries have also offered financial support for foster parents in these countries to take on orphaned children.

Supporters of international adoption maintain that the practice is in the best interest of the children. After all, what could be better than a loving, comfortable home with the resources to provide the care these children need to grow and prosper? According to human rights law, the child's best interest is paramount in such situations, and proponents of international adoptions assert that it is better for the child to find a loving, permanent home—even if it is half a world away—than to stay institutionalized in under-resourced orphanages or in foster families.

The debate over international adoption is a passionate one. Both proponents and critics claim that they only want the best situation for the child, but both have very different perspectives on how to reach that goal. The consequences of the international adoption debate are very real and impact millions of children around the globe and prospective parents who must navigate the confusing and often harsh adoption regulations in different countries.

The viewpoints in this chapter explore the debate over international adoption and whether the practice should or should not be encouraged. Other viewpoints in the chapter discuss the pros and cons of international adoptions of children orphaned by natural disasters, such as the tsunami in Indonesia, or in need of special care, such as the African AIDS orphans.

> *"Children's most fundamental human rights are to be raised in the families that are often available only internationally."*

International Adoptions Should Be Encouraged

Elizabeth Bartholet

Elizabeth Bartholet is the Morris Wasserstein Public Interest Professor of Law and Child Advocacy Program faculty director at Harvard University Law School. In the following viewpoint, she maintains that policies that prevent international adoptions are not only inhumane but also unjust. Bartholet argues that allowing and encouraging international adoptions is within the best interest of the child and that it is a fundamental human right for children to be adopted into loving homes.

As you read, consider the following questions:

1. What does core international human rights law proclaim in matters related to children and adoption?

2. What is the estimated number of orphaned children in the world?

3. How many million children are estimated to live in orphanages?

I flew from Boston, Massachusetts, to Lima, Peru, in 1985 to adopt the four-month-old who became Christopher, and flew back in 1987 to adopt the one-month-old who became Michael. I counted myself from the first moments they were put into my arms as extraordinarily lucky to be their parent.

But I still wondered at the policies that made it so hard to adopt. I spent three months in Lima for each adoption, enduring the most challenging experiences of my life. I nursed each child through terrifying illnesses, and agonized through endless sessions with police, social workers and courts. I fought off mysterious threats to remove the children who had become mine in every way except the law, threats that hung over us until the day we flew home.

I realized then that only a tiny fraction of those who might want to adopt a child from Peru would be able to. Few would have the kind of job I did, allowing an extended leave. Few would be able to deal with all the other difficulties of accomplishing a Peruvian adoption.

There Are Too Many Children in Need

I also began to learn how many children needed parents. Daily I would hear about those newly orphaned by the Shining Path [a Communist guerilla organization in Peru] terrorists. On visits to an orphanage, I saw babies crowding the nurseries, toddlers and older kids playing and fighting in the bleak yard, with its broken tricycles and swings. No system seemed to exist for terminating parental rights so children could be adopted, yet few of these children ever received a visit from a parent or other relative. The city's child welfare agency regularly told those who inquired about adoption that there were no children available.

I have spent much of the 25 years since these adoptions studying the needs of unparented children worldwide, and the role of international adoption. This has simply intensified my initial conviction that there is something terribly wrong with policies that lock children into orphanages, away from prospective parents.

For a period during this time, some more adoption-friendly policies developed. The Hague Convention on Intercountry Adoption [Convention on Protection of Children and Co-operation in Respect of Intercountry Adoption] was promulgated, preferring such adoption to in-country foster and institutional care. The numbers of international adoptions rose, reaching up to 45,000 worldwide. Some countries which had not allowed their children to be placed abroad opened up, including Russia, China, and countries in Eastern Europe and Africa. Adoption became less stigmatized, so that more people chose it as a way of having children.

However, now the world has reversed direction. The numbers of international adoptions have dropped dramatically. Many countries that had newly begun placing children abroad have closed again. Many have instituted restrictions requiring that children be held for long periods to explore in-country placement options, before any placement abroad. It is now almost unheard of for children to be placed internationally as the young infants that Christopher and Michael were. Indeed it is extremely rare for children under the age of one to be placed. Yet all familiar with developmental psychology and social science research know that keeping infants in institutional care for more than a few months puts them at enormous risk for lifelong damage, even if they are ultimately adopted, with the risk increased proportionately with the length of stay.

The organizations leading the attack on international adoption describe themselves as child human rights organizations. But human rights activism in its institutionalized form has often played a perverse role. Children's most fundamental human rights are to be raised in the families that are often available only internationally. . . .

Accepted Human Rights Principles Require That Children's Best Interests Govern

Core international human rights law proclaims that children's best interests should be the guiding principle in matters related to children and adoption. For example, Article 3 of the Convention on the Rights of the Child (CRC) provides generally that 'the best interest of the child shall be a primary consideration,' and Article 21 provides that in adoption it shall be 'the paramount consideration.' Article 1 of the Hague Convention on Intercountry Adoption provides that 'intercountry adoptions take place in the best interests of the child and with respect for his or her fundamental rights as recognized in international law.' Courts in South Africa, India, and Malawi have concluded that the CRC and related international human rights law make children's best interests determinative in cases involving international adoption. UNICEF [United Nations Children's Fund] and other critics of international adoption generally agree that children's best interests should govern, and thus focus their criticism on claims that children are injured by adoption abuses and by the loss of heritage rights involved in out-of-country placement.

If we take seriously the proposition that children's best interests must govern, there should be no dispute about how to resolve the central policy issues in international adoption.

International Adoption Serves Children's Most Basic Human Rights

Human beings need parental care for a prolonged period to survive physically and to develop mentally and emotionally. Even the best institutions fail to provide the kind of care that infants and young children need.

Key international laws proclaim the centrality of children's human rights to grow up in a family. The CRC preamble describes the family as 'the natural environment for the growth and well-being of . . . children.' The CRC and the Hague Convention on Intercountry Adoption include in their preambles that 'the child, for the full and harmonious development of his or her personality, should grow up in a family environment, in an atmosphere of happiness, love and understanding. . . .'

The CRC also provides that member states must give children who cannot be raised by their original parents adequate substitute care, and protect children against the conditions characteristic of institutional care. It says that an unparented child 'shall be entitled to special protection and assistance,' 'alternative care' (Article 20), and 'such protection and care as is necessary for his or her well-being' (Article 3). It says that 'every child has the inherent right to life,' and to 'survival and development' (Article 6). It grants children affirmative rights to health, a standard of living adequate for appropriate development, and education (Articles 24, 27, and 28). It requires states to 'protect the child from all forms of physical or mental violence, injury or abuse, neglect or negligent treatment, maltreatment or exploitation' (Article 19). It provides that 'no child shall be subjected to torture or other cruel, inhuman or degrading treatment,' nor 'deprived of his or her liberty unlawfully or arbitrarily' (Article 37).

Right for True Family Care

Accordingly, core human rights principles support the proposition that children have a right to be raised by parents who can provide true family care. Unparented children have a right to be placed in international adoption if that is where homes are available. They have a right to be liberated from the conditions characterizing orphanages, street life, and most foster care.

Courts have recognized these principles in decisions involving international adoption. Justice [P.N.] Bhagwati in a 1984 case in India found a right to international adoption despite the absence of statutory recognition of such adoption, relying on international human rights law and related provisions in the Indian Constitution. He reasoned:

[C]hildren need special protection because of their tender age and physique, mental immaturity and incapacity to look after themselves. That is why there is a growing realization in every part of the globe that children must be brought up in an atmosphere of love and affection and under the tender care and attention of parents so that they may be able to attain full emotional, intellectual and spiritual stability and maturity. . . .

. . . Every child has a right to love and be loved and to grow up in an atmosphere of love and affection and of moral and material security and this is possible only if the child is brought up in a family. . . . [I]f for any reason it is not possible for the biological parents or other near relative to look after the child . . . , the next best alternative would be to find adoptive parents. . . .

. . . [I]f it is not possible to provide them in India decent family life where they can grow up under the loving care and attention of parents . . . , there is no reason why such children should not be allowed to be given in adoption to foreign parents. (*Lakshmi Kant Pandey v. Union of India*, 1984, pp. 474, 476)

The Malawi High Court, in upholding [celebrity entertainer] Madonna's first adoption despite the residence requirement read by some to forbid international adoption, also relied on international human rights law, both the CRC and the African Charter on the Rights and Welfare of the Child. It granted her adoption of David Banda based on finding that Madonna offered the true home that was unavailable in Malawi:

The reality of the situation in Malawi is that a lot of children are in dire situation of material deprivation characterized by poverty, lack of access to essential nutrition, lack of access to education, lack of access to proper sanitation and lack of access to adequate health care. This is the inescapable reality in Malawi as in most third world countries. And to argue that we will soon find adequate solutions for all our deprived children is to assert a shameless and insolent lie.

The infant in the instant case was among our many materially deprived children whose only remaining parent was forced, because of his circumstances, to place him at an orphanage. . . . In seeking to adopt the infant the petitioners are not therefore in the way of any permanent domestic solution for the infant.

Madonna's Second International Adoption

The Malawi Supreme Court of Appeal granting Madonna's second adoption, involving 'Mercy' James, relied on similar international human rights law:

We do not think that under [Malawi law] inter-country adoption is a last resort alternative. . . . [S]ince the case of infant CJ surfaced itself there has not been a single family in Malawi that has come forward to adopt infant CJ neither have there been any attempt by anybody to place infant CJ in a foster family. . . . [T]here are only two options. She can either stay in Kondanani Orphanage and have no family life at all or she can be adopted by the Appellant and grow in a family. . . . In our Judgment the welfare of infant CJ will be better taken care of by having her adopted by the foreign parent rather than for her to grow up in an orphanage where she will have no family life, no love and affection of parents.

The Constitutional Court of South Africa stated in a 2007 decision by Justice [Albie] Sachs approving an international adoption, that the CRC 'seems to accept the notion that "[e]nsuring that a child grows up in a loving, permanent home is the ultimate form of care a country can bestow upon a child" even if that result is achieved through an inter-country adoption.'

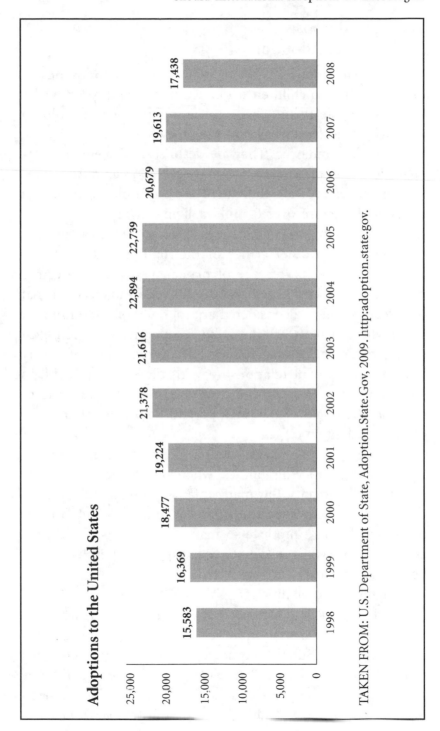

Adoptions to the United States

Year	Adoptions
1998	15,583
1999	16,369
2000	18,477
2001	19,224
2002	21,378
2003	21,616
2004	22,894
2005	22,739
2006	20,679
2007	19,613
2008	17,438

TAKEN FROM: U.S. Department of State, Adoption.State.Gov, 2009. http:adoption.state.gov.

The Core Purpose of International Adoption

International adoption is about placing tens of thousands of infants and young children who need homes with people who want to provide them. There are many millions of children worldwide who need homes because they have been orphaned, abandoned, or removed. They are destined to live either in orphanages or on the streets if they are not adopted internationally. Estimates indicate that there are 143 million orphaned children. There are over 8 million living in orphanages, and some 100 million street children with no available caregivers.

UNICEF and other critics of international adoption say that only a small percentage of orphanage children are true orphans in the sense that both parents are dead, arguing that only these should be considered appropriate for adoption. But those whose parents are not dead have either been removed for maltreatment or abandoned. The overwhelming majority have no meaningful relationship with their parents, and no likelihood of ever returning home. It is in the interests of these children, and of the birth parents who love them, to be placed in adoption.

UNICEF and others also say that most orphanage children are older and suffer disabilities, whereas prospective adopters prefer healthy infants. But many infants are placed in orphanages. It is restrictive adoption policies and the conditions of orphanage life that produce so many older children with disabilities. And while prospective adopters generally prefer healthy infants, many are interested in adopting older children with significant disabilities.

At their peak in 2004, international adoptions reached up to 45,000. This is a small number by comparison to those in need of homes. But the homes make a huge difference for those placed. And the number could easily be multiplied many times if we developed policies facilitating rather than restricting placement. Surveys show that significant percentages of adults in privileged countries are interested in adopting. Some 9.9 million of 'ever married' women in the U.S. alone have considered adoption, and only one percent of these adopt in a given year.

No Question What Is Better for Children

The contrast between the homes international adoption offers and orphanage or street life is so extreme as to make unnecessary any debate as to what best serves children's human rights. Most orphanages are terrible places, where children learn not to cry because crying brings no response. A recent article describes a typical institution for children under three in Bulgaria:

> It is the smell that [first] assaults you—filthy nappies [diapers], unwashed babies, rotting flesh. Then you are hit by the silence, an eerie, unnatural silence, the silence of babies who have given up hope of ever being consoled, cuddled or comforted. It is the dreadful quiet of starving, neglected, unloved children waiting to die. . . . The children in this particular wing have no human contact. They are fed lying on their backs, and have their nappies changed only when there happens to be a supply of new ones. Not one single word is uttered to them, so none of them is able to talk. This is how they live, and this is how they die. . . . These children are Europe's guilty secret, hidden away from the world.

Studies document how destructive orphanage conditions are, even in the better orphanages, producing lifelong emotional and intellectual damage even for many of those children lucky enough to be eventually adopted. Developmental psychologists explain how essential nurturing human interaction is for infants to develop normally. The new science of early brain development demonstrates in dramatic color slides how differently the brains of children raised for two years in an orphanage look as compared to the brains of children raised with parents. The World Health Organization recommends that even 'when high-quality institutions are used as an emergency measure ... the length of stay should be no more than 3 months.'

Adoption as a Human Rights Issue

Street children often die early, and those that live suffer maltreatment, disease, exploitation for sex, labor and child soldiering, and trafficking for sex and forced labor in other countries. International adoption provides the only hope for a loving and nurturing home for most children in need, as discussed above. And international adoption produces good homes that work well for children. Studies show that those placed in early infancy do essentially as well as non-adopted children. For children who have suffered terrible damage by virtue of wartime trauma or orphanage life, the studies show international adoption does much to overcome deficits, enabling many to live essentially normal lives.

Financial Aspects of International Adoptions

And the expenses for international adoption are paid by adoptive parents. Neither sending nor receiving countries need divert significant resources to finance such adoption. Sending countries are relieved of the costs of institutionalization for all those placed, freeing up resources to serve the needs of other children. International adoption also produces significant additional resources for poor countries and their people. Adoptive parents pay fees to agencies and orphanages, some of which go to improve orphanage conditions. China charges an orphanage fee for each adoption of $3000–5000. Given the 7900 children adopted into the U.S. from China in 2005, and assuming the minimum $3000 fee, this meant $23,700,000 to improve orphanage conditions.

Some critics of international adoption have argued for a systematic tax on such adoption, charging adoptive parents an extra few thousand dollars per adoption to support family preservation in sending countries. But this would limit the chances for children to get adoptive homes, since raising the price of adoption will deter potential adopters.

In any event, there is ample evidence that the experience of adopting children from other countries triggers significant voluntary contributions by individuals and agencies to improve conditions in sending countries, in the absence of any such tax. And the exposure international adoption brings creates new consciousness about these countries' problems more broadly, and thus the potential for a wide range of helpful action by individuals and governments.

One example among thousands of the productive interaction between international adoption and broader reform, is the work of Dr. Jane Aronson, whose understanding of the problems suffered by orphanage children began with her work as a pediatrician for international adoptive families. Dr. Aronson has worked on her own and with one of her adoptive parents, [celebrity actress] Angelina Jolie, to develop and fund several organizations that serve the needs of more than 10,000 children worldwide, building foster care and improving orphanage conditions. Her 'Orphan Rangers' provides visits to orphanage children who would otherwise experience no loving human contact.

The Malawi Supreme Court that approved Madonna's second adoption recognized the interaction between her two adoptions and the many millions she had donated to improve conditions for other poor children in Malawi. It noted, in concluding that she satisfied Malawi's residence requirement:

> [T]he Appellant is not a mere sojourner in this country but has a targeted long-term presence aimed at ameliorating the lives of more disadvantaged children in Malawi.... [S]he is not here only to adopt infant CJ but to also implement her long-term ideas of investing in the improvement of more

children's lives with her projects in Malawi. In our view it is clear that ... [she] was at the time of this application resident in Malawi.

> "Unless we recognize that behind the altruistic veneer, international adoption has become an industry—one that is often highly lucrative and sometimes corrupt—many more adoption stories will have unhappy endings."

International Adoptions Should Be Discouraged

E.J. Graff

E.J. Graff is an author and a journalist who is an associate director and senior researcher at the Schuster Institute for Investigative Journalism at Brandeis University. In the following viewpoint, Graff contends that the prevailing notion that thousands of infants and toddlers are waiting to be adopted by Americans is a myth. The real story, Graff argues, is that the supply of healthy babies does not meet the overwhelming demand and often results in child abduction and trafficking, aided by corrupt adoption and government officials.

As you read, consider the following questions:

1. How many children from developing countries were adopted by foreigners in 2004?

2. Americans adopted how many of every 110 Guatemalan children born in 2006?

3. What is the aim of the Hague Convention on Intercountry Adoption?

We all know the story of international adoption: Millions of infants and toddlers have been abandoned or orphaned—placed on the side of a road or on the doorstep of a church, or left parentless due to AIDS, destitution, or war. These little ones find themselves forgotten, living in crowded orphanages or ending up on the streets, facing an uncertain future of misery and neglect. But, if they are lucky, adoring new moms and dads from faraway lands whisk them away for a chance at a better life.

Unfortunately, this story is largely fiction.

The Real Story

Westerners have been sold the myth of a world orphan crisis. We are told that millions of children are waiting for their "forever families" to rescue them from lives of abandonment and abuse. But many of the infants and toddlers being adopted by Western parents today are not orphans at all. Yes, hundreds of thousands of children around the world do need loving homes. But more often than not, the neediest children are sick, disabled, traumatized, or older than 5. They are not the healthy babies that, quite understandably, most Westerners hope to adopt. There are simply not enough healthy, adoptable infants to meet Western demand—and there's too much Western money in search of children. As a result, many international adoption agencies work not to find homes for needy children but to find children for Western homes.

Since the mid-1990s, the number of international adoptions each year has nearly doubled, from 22,200 in 1995 to just under 40,000 in 2006. At its peak, in 2004, more than 45,000 children from developing countries were adopted by foreigners. Americans bring home more of these children than any other nationality—more than half the global total in recent years.

Where do these babies come from? As international adoptions have flourished, so has evidence that babies in many countries are being systematically bought, coerced, and stolen away from their birth families. Nearly half the 40 countries listed by the U.S. State Department as the top sources for international adoption over the past 15 years—places such as Belarus, Brazil, Ethiopia, Honduras, Peru, and Romania—have at least temporarily halted adoptions or been prevented from sending children to the United States because of serious concerns about corruption and kidnapping. And yet when a country is closed due to corruption, many adoption agencies simply transfer their clients' hopes to the next "hot" country. That country abruptly experiences a spike in infants and toddlers adopted overseas—until it too is forced to shut its doors.

Along the way, the international adoption industry has become a market often driven by its customers. Prospective adoptive parents in the United States will pay adoption agencies between $15,000 and $35,000 (excluding travel, visa costs, and other miscellaneous expenses) for the chance to bring home a little one. Special needs or older children can be adopted at a discount. Agencies claim the costs pay for the agency's fee, the cost of foreign salaries and operations, staff travel, and orphanage donations. But experts say the fees are so disproportionately large for the child's home country that they encourage corruption.

To complicate matters further, while international adoption has become an industry driven by money, it is also charged with strong emotions. Many adoption agencies and adoptive parents passionately insist that crooked practices are not systemic, but tragic, isolated cases. Arrest the bad guys, they say, but let the "good" adoptions continue. However, remove cash from the adoption chain, and, outside of China, the number of healthy babies needing Western homes all but disappears. Nigel Cantwell, a Geneva-based consultant on child protection policy, has seen the dangerous influence of money on adoptions in Eastern Europe and Central Asia, where he has helped reform corrupt adoption systems. In these regions, healthy children age 3 and younger can easily be adopted in their own countries, he says. I asked him how many healthy babies in those regions would be available for international adoption if money never exchanged hands. "I would hazard a guess at zero," he replied.

The Myth of Supply

International adoption wasn't always a demand-driven industry. Half a century ago, it was primarily a humanitarian effort for children orphaned by conflict. In 1955, news spread that Bertha and Harry Holt, an evangelical couple from Oregon, had adopted eight Korean War orphans, and families across the United States expressed interest in following their example. Since then, international adoption has become increasingly popular in Australia, Canada, Europe, and the United States. Americans adopted more than 20,000 foreign children in 2006 alone, up from just 8,987 in 1995. Half a dozen European countries regularly bring home more foreign-born children per capita than does the United States. Today, Canada, France, Italy, Spain, and the United States account for 4 out of every 5 international adoptions.

Changes in Western demography explain much of the growth. Thanks to contraception, abortion, and delayed marriages, the number of unplanned births in most developed countries has declined in recent decades. Some women who delay having children discover they've outwaited their fertility; others have difficulty conceiving from the beginning. Still others adopt for religious reasons, explaining that they've been called to care for children in need. In the United States, a motive beyond demography is the notion that international adoption is somehow "safer"—more predictable and more likely to end in success—than many domestic adoptions, where there's an outsized fear of a birth mother's last-minute change of heart. Add an ocean of distance, and the idea that needy children abound in poor countries, and that risk seems to disappear.

But international adoptions are no less risky; they're simply less regulated. Just as companies outsource industry to countries with lax labor laws and low wages, adoptions have moved to states with few laws about the process. Poor, illiterate birth parents in the developing world simply have fewer protections than their counterparts in the United States, especially in countries where human trafficking and corruption are rampant. And too often, these imbalances are overlooked on the adopting end. After all, one country after another has continued to supply what adoptive parents want most.

In reality, there are very few young, healthy orphans available for adoption around the world. Orphans are rarely healthy babies; healthy babies are rarely orphaned. "It's not really true," says Alexandra Yuster, a senior advisor on child protection with UNICEF [United Nations Children's Fund], "that there are large numbers of infants with no homes who either will be in institutions or who need intercountry adoption."

Who Is to Blame?

That assertion runs counter to the story line that has long been marketed to Americans and other Westerners, who have been trained by images of destitution in developing countries and the seemingly endless flow of daughters from China to believe that millions of orphaned babies around the world desperately need homes. UNICEF itself is partly responsible for this erroneous assumption. The organization's statistics on orphans and institutionalized children are widely quoted to justify the need for international adoption. In 2006, UNICEF reported an estimated 132 million orphans in sub-Saharan Africa, Asia, Latin America, and the Caribbean. But the organization's definition of "orphan" includes children who have lost just one parent, either to desertion or death. Just 10 percent of the total—13 million children—have lost both parents, and most of these live with extended family. They are also older: By UNICEF's own estimate, 95 percent of orphans are older than 5. In other words, UNICEF's "millions of orphans" are not healthy babies doomed to institutional misery unless Westerners adopt and save them. Rather, they are mostly older children living with extended families who need financial support.

The exception is China, where the country's three-decades-old one-child policy, now being loosened, has created an unprecedented number of girls available for adoption. But even this flow of daughters is finite; China has far more hopeful foreigners looking to adopt a child than it has orphans it is willing to send overseas. In 2005, foreign parents adopted nearly 14,500 Chinese children. That was far fewer than the number of Westerners who wanted to adopt; adoption agencies report many more clients waiting in line. And taking those children home has gotten harder; in 2007, China's central adoption authority sharply reduced the number of children sent abroad, possibly because of the country's growing sex imbalance, declining poverty, and scandals involving child trafficking for foreign adoption. Prospective foreign parents today are strictly judged by their age, marital history, family size, income, health, and even weight. That means that if you are single, gay, fat, old, less than well off, too often divorced, too recently married, taking antidepressants, or already have four children, China will turn you away. Even those allowed a spot in line are being told they might wait three to four years before they bring home a child. That has led many prospective parents to shop around for a country that puts fewer barriers between them and their children—as if every country were China, but with fewer onerous regulations.

The Case of Guatemala

One such country has been Guatemala, which in 2006 and 2007 was the No. 2 exporter of children to the United States. Between 1997 and 2006, the number of Guatemalan children adopted by Americans more than quadrupled, to more than 4,500 annually. Incredibly, in 2006, American parents adopted one of every 110 Guatemalan children born. In 2007, nearly 9 out of 10 children adopted were less than a year old; almost half were younger than 6 months old. "Guatemala is a perfect case study of how international adoption has become a demand-driven business," says Kelley McCreery Bunkers, a former consultant with UNICEF Guatemala. The country's adoption process was "an industry developed to meet the needs of adoptive families in developed countries, specifically the United States."

Because the vast majority of the country's institutionalized children are not healthy, adoptable babies, almost none have been adopted abroad. In the fall of 2007, a survey conducted by the Guatemalan government, UNICEF, and the international child welfare and adoption agency Holt International Children's Services found approximately 5,600 children and adolescents in Guatemalan institutions. More than 4,600 of these children were age 4 or older. Fewer than 400 were under a year old. And yet in 2006, more than 270 Guatemalan babies, all younger than 12 months, were being sent to the United States each month. These adopted children were simply not coming from the country's institutions. Last year [2007], 98 percent of U.S. adoptions from Guatemala were "relinquishments": Babies who had never seen the inside of an institution were signed over directly to a private attorney who approved the international adoption—for a very considerable fee—without any review by a judge or social service agency.

So, where had some of these adopted babies come from? Consider the case of Ana Escobar, a young Guatemalan woman who in March 2007 reported to police that armed men had locked her in a closet in her family's shoe store and stolen her infant. After a 14-month search, Escobar found her daughter in pre-adoption foster care, just weeks before the girl was to be adopted by a couple from Indiana. DNA testing showed the toddler to be Escobar's child. In a similar case from 2006, Raquel Par, another Guatemalan woman, reported being drugged while waiting for a bus in Guatemala City, waking to find her year-old baby missing. Three months later, Par learned her daughter had been adopted by an American couple.

On Jan. 1, 2008, Guatemala closed its doors to American adoptions so that the government could reform the broken process. Britain, Canada, France, Germany, the Netherlands, and Spain all stopped accepting adoptions from the country several years earlier, citing trafficking concerns. But more than 2,280 American adoptions from the country are still being processed, albeit with additional safeguards. Stolen babies have already been found in that queue; Guatemalan authorities expect more.

Corruption Is Widespread

Guatemala's example is extreme; it is widely considered to have the world's most notorious record of corruption in foreign adoption. But the same troubling trends have emerged, on smaller scales, in more than a dozen other countries, including Albania, Cambodia, Ethiopia, Liberia, Peru, and Vietnam. The pattern suggests that the supply of adoptable babies rises to meet foreign demand—and disappears when Western cash is no longer available. For instance, in December 2001, the U.S. immigration service stopped processing adoption visas from Cambodia, citing clear evidence that children were being acquired illicitly, often against their parents' wishes. That year, Westerners adopted more than 700 Cambodian children; of the 400 adopted by Americans, more than half were less than 12 months old. But in 2005, a study of Cambodia's orphanage population, commissioned by the U.S.

Agency for International Development, found only a total of 132 children who were less than a year old—fewer babies than Westerners had been adopting every three months a few years before.

Even countries with large populations, such as India, rarely have healthy infants and toddlers who need foreign parents. India's large and growing middle class, at home and in the diaspora, faces fertility issues like those of their developed-world counterparts. They too are looking for healthy babies to adopt; some experts think that these millions of middle-class families could easily absorb all available babies. The country's pervasive poverty does leave many children fending for themselves on the street. But "kids are not on the street alone at the age of 2," Cantwell, the child protection consultant, says. "They are 5 or 6, and they aren't going to be adopted." That's partly because most of these children still have family ties and therefore are not legally available for adoption, and partly because they would have difficulty adjusting to a middle-class European or North American home. Many of these children are deeply marked by abuse, crime, and poverty, and few prospective parents are prepared to adopt them.

Surely, though, prospective parents can at least feel secure that their child is truly an orphan in need of a home if they receive all the appropriate legal papers? Unfortunately, no.

Nursery Crimes

In many countries, it can be astonishingly easy to fabricate a history for a young child, and in the process, manufacture an orphan. The birth mothers are often poor, young, unmarried, divorced, or otherwise lacking family protection. The children may be born into a locally despised minority group that is afforded few rights. And for enough money, someone will separate these little ones from their vulnerable families, turning them into "paper orphans" for lucrative export.

Some manufactured orphans are indeed found in what Westerners call "orphanages." But these establishments often serve less as homes to parentless children and more as boarding schools for poor youngsters. Many children are there only temporarily, seeking food, shelter, and education while their parents, because of poverty or illness, cannot care for them. Many families visit their children, or even bring them home on weekends, until they can return home permanently. In 2005, when the Hannah B. Williams Orphanage in Monrovia, Liberia, was closed because of shocking living conditions, 89 of the 102 "orphans" there returned to their families. In Vietnam, "rural families in particular will put their babies into these orphanages that are really extended day care centers during the harvest season," says a U.S. Embassy spokeswoman in Hanoi. In some cases, unscrupulous orphanage directors, local officials, or other operators persuade illiterate birth families to sign documents that relinquish those children, who are then sent abroad for adoption, never to be seen again by their bereft families.

Other children are located through similarly nefarious means. Western adoption agencies often contract with in-country facilitators—sometimes orphanage directors, sometimes freelancers—and pay per-child fees for each healthy baby adopted. These facilitators, in turn, subcontract with child finders, often for sums in vast excess of local wages. These paydays give individuals a significant financial incentive to find adoptable babies at almost any cost. In Guatemala, where the GDP [gross domestic product] per capita is $4,700 a year, child finders often earned $6,000 to $8,000 for each healthy, adoptable infant. In many cases, child finders simply paid poor families for infants. A May 2007 report on adoption trafficking by the Hague Conference on Private International Law reported poor Guatemalan families being paid between $300 and several thousand dollars per child.

Medical Industry Is Involved

Sometimes, medical professionals serve as child finders to obtain infants. In Vietnam, for instance, a finder's fee for a single child can easily dwarf a nurse's $50-a-month salary. Some nurses and doctors coerce birth mothers into giving up their children by offering them a choice: pay outrageously inflated hospital bills or relinquish their newborns. Illiterate new mothers are made to sign documents they can't read. In August 2008, the U.S. State Department released a warning that birth certificates issued by Tu Du Hospital in Ho Chi Minh City—which in 2007 had reported 200 births a day, and an average of three abandoned babies per 100 births—were "unreliable." Most of the hospital's "abandoned" babies were sent to the city's Tam Binh orphanage, from which many Westerners have adopted. (Tu Du Hospital is where [celebrity actress] Angelina Jolie's Vietnamese-born son was reportedly abandoned one month after his birth; he was at Tam Binh when she adopted him.) According to Linh Song, executive director of Ethica, an American nonprofit devoted to promoting ethical adoption, a provincial hospital's chief obstetrician told her in 2007 "that he provided 10 ethnic minority infants to [an] orphanage [for adoption] in return for an incubator."

To smooth the adoption process, officials in the children's home countries may be bribed to create false identity documents. Consular officials for the adopting countries generally accept whatever documents they receive. But if a local U.S. Embassy has seen a series of worrisome referrals—say, a sudden spike in healthy infants coming from the same few orphanages, or a single province sending an unusually high number of babies with suspiciously similar paperwork—officials may investigate. But generally, they do not want to obstruct adoptions of genuinely needy children or get in the way of people longing for a child. However, many frequently doubt that the adoptions crossing their desks are completely aboveboard. "I believe in intercountry adoption very strongly," says

Katherine Monahan, a U.S. State Department official who has overseen scores of U.S. adoptions from around the world. "[But] I worry that there were many children that could have stayed with their families if we could have provided them with even a little economic assistance." One U.S. official told me that when embassy staff in a country that sent more than 1,000 children overseas last year were asked which adoption visas they felt uneasy about, they replied: almost all of them.

Most of the Westerners involved with foreign adoption agencies—like businesspeople importing foreign sneakers—can plausibly deny knowledge of unethical or unseemly practices overseas. They don't have to know. Willful ignorance allowed Lauryn Galindo, a former hula dancer from the United States, to collect more than $9 million in adoption fees over several years for Cambodian infants and toddlers. Between 1997 and 2001, Americans adopted 1,230 children from Cambodia; Galindo said she was involved in 800 of the adoptions. (Galindo reportedly delivered Angelina Jolie's Cambodian child to her movie set in Africa.) But in a two-year probe beginning in 2002, U.S. investigators alleged that Galindo paid Cambodian child finders to purchase, defraud, coerce, or steal children from their families, and conspired to create false identity documents for the children. Galindo later served federal prison time on charges of visa fraud and money laundering, but not trafficking. "You can get away with buying babies around the world as a United States citizen," says Richard Cross, a senior special agent with U.S. Immigration and Customs Enforcement who investigated Galindo. "It's not a crime."

Rocking the Cradle

Buying a child abroad is something most prospective parents want no part of. So, how can it be prevented? As international adoption has grown in the past decade, the ad hoc approach of closing some corrupt countries to adoption and shifting parents' hopes (and money) to the next destination has failed.

The agencies that profit from adoption appear to willfully ignore how their own payments and fees are causing both the corruption and the closures.

Some countries that send children overseas for adoption have kept the process lawful and transparent from nearly the beginning and their model is instructive. Thailand, for instance, has a central government authority that counsels birth mothers and offers some families social and economic support so that poverty is never a reason to give up a child. Other countries, such as Paraguay and Romania, reformed their processes after sharp surges in shady adoptions in the 1990s. But those reforms were essentially to stop international adoptions almost entirely. In 1994, Paraguay sent 483 children to the United States; last year, the country sent none.

For a more comprehensive solution, the best hope may be the Hague Convention on Intercountry Adoption [Convention on Protection of Children and Co-operation in Respect of Intercountry Adoption], an international agreement designed to prevent child trafficking for adoption. On April 1, 2008, the United States formally entered the agreement, which has 75 other signatories. In states that send children overseas and are party to the convention, such as Albania, Bulgaria, Colombia, and the Philippines, Hague-compatible reforms have included a central government authority overseeing child welfare, efforts to place needy children with extended families and local communities first, and limits on the number of foreign adoption agencies authorized to work in the country. The result, according to experts, has been a sharp decline in baby buying, fraud, coercion, and kidnapping for adoption.

In adopting countries, the convention requires a central authority—in the United States' case, the State Department—to oversee international adoption. The State Department empowers two nonprofit organizations to certify adoption agencies; if shady practices, fraud, financial improprieties, or links with trafficking come to light, accreditation can be revoked. Already, the rules appear to be having some effect: Several U.S. agencies long dogged by rumors of bad practices have been denied accreditation; some have shut their doors. But no international treaty is perfect, and the Hague Convention is no exception. Many of the countries sending their children to the West, including Ethiopia, Russia, South Korea, Ukraine, and Vietnam, have yet to join the agreement.

More Regulation Would Help

Perhaps most important, more effective regulations would strictly limit the amount of money that changes hands. Per-child fees could be outlawed. Payments could be capped to cover only legitimate costs such as medical care, food, and clothing for the children. And crucially, fees must be kept proportionate with the local economies. "Unless you control the money, you won't control the corruption," says Thomas Di-Filipo, president of the Joint Council on International Children's Services, which represents more than 200 international adoption organizations. "If we have the greatest laws and the greatest regulations but are still sending $20,000 anywhere—well, you can bypass any system with enough cash."

Improved regulations will protect not only the children being adopted and their birth families, but also the consumers: hopeful parents. Adopting a child—like giving birth—is an emotional experience; it can be made wrenching by the abhorrent realization that a child believed to be an orphan simply isn't. One American who adopted a little girl from Cambodia in 2002 wept as she spoke at an adoption ethics conference in October 2007 about such a discovery. "I was told she was an orphan," she said. "One year after she came home, and she could speak English well enough, she told me about her mommy and daddy and her brothers and her sisters."

Unless we recognize that behind the altruistic veneer, international adoption has become an industry—one that is often highly lucrative and sometimes corrupt—many more adoption stories will have unhappy endings. Unless adoption agencies are held to account, more young children will be wrongfully taken from their families. And unless those desperate to become parents demand reform, they will continue—wittingly or not—to pay for wrongdoing. "Credulous Westerners eager to believe that they are saving children are easily fooled into accepting laundered children," writes David Smolin, a law professor and advocate for international adoption reform. "For there is no fool like the one who wants to be fooled."

> "Historically, the practice of intercountry adoption has been a humanitarian response to the plight of children in the aftermath of armed conflicts, political and economic crises, and social upheavals."

International Adoptions Should Be an Option for Tsunami Orphans

Evan B. Donaldson Adoption Institute

The Evan B. Donaldson Adoption Institute is a national non-profit organization established to improve adoption laws and practices. In the following viewpoint, the Adoption Institute delineates the role of international adoption in situations of armed conflict, natural disasters, and other serious human emergencies. It also outlines the needs of children during such situations as well as the measures countries should take to protect children from exploitation and child trafficking during dire emergencies.

As you read, consider the following questions:

1. What is the number of estimated dead as a result of the December 2004 tsunami in Southeast Asia?

2. How many children have been identified as either having been separated from or having lost one or both parents as a result of the tsunami?

3. What steps has Indonesia taken to protect children affected by the tsunami?

People and organizations around the world responded with an enormous outpouring of concern and assistance after the massive tsunami that struck Southeast Asia and the eastern coast of Africa on Dec. 26, 2004. It is now estimated that the tsunami, although not the largest in recorded history, has inflicted some of the greatest devastation, claiming more than 170,000 lives and displacing an estimated 1.5 million people. As it became clear that a large portion of those most affected were children, many Americans (and would-be parents from other nations) were moved to open their hearts and homes—through adoption—to the boys and girls who seemed to have been orphaned.

In response to the enormous number of inquiries, the U.S. State Department—as well as numerous European governments, international and nongovernmental organizations (NGOs), and agencies involved in intercountry adoptions—announced that they opposed adoptions from the areas hit by the tsunami. The State Department explicitly stated that no adoptions would occur until those countries were stabilized to the point where legitimate orphans could be identified and, even then, that adoptions would take place only in nations that "decide to make these orphans available for international adoption."

The Evan B. Donaldson Adoption Institute shares in mourning the tragic loss of life caused by the tsunami. And, like so many others, the Institute is concerned about the fate of the thousands of boys and girls who now face uncertain futures as a result of the deaths of one or both of their parents. Because there has been widespread discussion about whether these children should be adopted, the Adoption Institute offers this [viewpoint], with the purpose of examining the role of intercountry adoption in situations such as the one caused by the tsunami—that is, during natural disasters, armed conflicts, and other complex human emergencies.

By outlining some of the unique threats posed to children during emergencies, and examining existing international conventions and the legal framework for intercountry adoption, it is the Institute's intent to articulate best practices that incorporate both immediate and long-term needs of children left without parental care—including protection, family reunification, community and family solutions, permanency, and respect of culture. We hope this [viewpoint] will stimulate dialogue among adoption professionals, policy makers, international organizations, and NGOs involved in providing humanitarian aid during crises, and will highlight the need to establish high ethical and practice standards among all parties interested in the welfare of children during such times.

Needs of Children in Emergencies

It is well known that during emergencies—in particular armed conflicts—basic infrastructure such as health, education, water and sanitation, as well as communication, may be undermined or destroyed; under-resourced governments may have little control or ability to manage the crisis; communities may be compromised or limited as a result of psychological trauma, destruction of material resources and population displacement; and societal values may break down, leading to an increase in criminal and antisocial behavior. As a result, the risk to children is greatly heightened because the protective environment of family, community, and government is compromised. Boys and girls who are unaccompanied and/or separated from primary caregivers may be more vulnerable to child trafficking, labor and sexual exploitation, or recruitment as child soldiers. In addition, traditional forms of alternative out-of-home care for children without parents may not be sufficient.

Indeed, these threats to children in the immediate aftermath of the tsunami were evident in confirmed reports by the United Nations Children's Fund (UNICEF) of a child being trafficked in the hardest hit province of Aceh, Indonesia, and of adolescent boys and girls being recruited as soldiers by the Tamil Tiger rebels [Liberation Tigers of Tamil Eelam] in Sri Lanka. In Sri Lanka, approximately 90 percent of the people internally displaced by the tsunami had been uprooted before as a result of the ethnic conflict and civil war that has ravaged the country for 18 years. For more than a decade, there has been a rebellion of Muslim separatists in the province of Aceh, Indonesia. In response to fears that children could be exploited or abducted by human traffickers—a problem throughout the region—Sri Lanka banned the adoption of any child affected by the tsunami either for in-country or intercountry adoption, while Indonesia banned the transfer of any child under the age of 16 from the most devastated province of Aceh, and explicitly banned any intercountry adoptions.

The challenge of caring for and protecting children in an emergency can be further complicated by the sheer number of boys and girls affected. In the 1994 genocide in Rwanda, for instance, about a half million—nearly one-fifth of all children in the population—lost one or both parents, and in the 2003 earthquake in Bam, Iran, up to 1,500 children lost their parents. Currently, as a result of the tsunami, nearly 10,000 children have been identified as either having been separated from or having lost one or both parents. Although these numbers are likely to increase as the situations of children are further clarified, they are not likely to reach the tens of thousands of orphans that were initially estimated, reflecting the tragic fact that the majority of children believed to have survived were, instead, swept to their deaths.

International Framework for the Protection of Children and Ethical Adoption Practice

Ethical principles for protecting the lives and rights of children, as they relate to adoption, have been set forth in a number of international declarations (which are legally nonbinding) and conventions (which are binding). These include:

- 1980 Convention on International Child Abduction [Hague Convention on the Civil Aspects of International Child Abduction]

- 1986 United Nations [UN] Declaration on Social and Legal Principles Relating to the Protection and Welfare of Children, with Special Reference to Foster Placement and Adoption Nationally and Internationally (the UN Declaration)

- 1989 UN Convention on the Rights of the Child (CRC) and its two Optional Protocols (2000)

- 1993 Hague Convention on Protection of Children and Co-operation in Respect of Intercountry Adoption (the Hague Convention) and its Recommendation on Displaced Children (1994).

In addition, a number of organizations have developed guidelines for ethical practice and the care of children who have been separated from parents and extended family. The following is a compilation of "best practices" regarding the care of children in the immediate aftermath of emergencies, based on widely accepted ethical adoption practice and international conventions:

Protection of Children

In the immediate aftermath of a crisis or emergency, priority should be given to the safety and security of children and to keeping them alive by providing access to clean water, adequate sanitation, basic nutrition, routine medical care and shelter. Article 35 of the CRC specifically states that adequate protection from sale, trafficking and abduction of children must be ensured, and the Hague Convention sets up a mechanism for international cooperation through a system of national Central Authorities in order to prevent the abduction, sale, or trafficking of children.

Family and Reunification

Children who are unaccompanied or separated from primary caregivers as the result of an emergency may not necessarily be orphans; thus, an effort to trace family members is vital. The Hague Convention requires that eligibility for adoption be determined by competent authorities. In the aftermath of an emergency, governments may not be able to ensure that appropriate consents for relinquishments for adoption are carried out or that a child is truly orphaned. The United Nations High Commissioner for Refugees (UNHCR) stipulates two years as a "reasonable period" to trace parents or other surviving family members (UNHCR, 1995).

Family and Community Solutions

Even during emergencies, institutions should be viewed as a last resort, and should be used only when children genuinely have no one to take care of them. Residential institutions rarely provide the care necessary for normative child development or protection. Although some institutions will be necessary to care for children's immediate needs, they should be used with the clear objective of providing temporary services while reunification or alternative community- and family based care is obtained

Widespread Trauma

Particularly during an emergency, it is necessary to address the widespread trauma caused by witnessing or directly experiencing brutal events. All children who have experienced trauma are vulnerable, but for children separated from their families, there is additional critical loss. The best way to help a child mitigate the effects of trauma is to restore a sense of normalcy by providing structured activities, care and nurturing. Children who have experienced traumatic events, at least in the short term, generally should not be further uprooted and placed in new environments.

Respect for Nation, Culture and Religion

Even though some children may be identified as parentless, there are countries that do not recognize adoption—for instance because of the Islamic Sharia law. Moreover, the right of a child to be raised in his or her family of origin is stipulated in Article 17 of the UN Declaration, Article 21 of the Convention on the Rights of the Child (CRC), and in the preamble of the Hague Convention. Article 16 of the Hague Convention requires that due consideration be given to "the child's upbringing and his or her ethnic, religious and cultural background."

Intercountry Adoption: When Is It a Solution?

It is clear that current international conventions and ethical adoption practice guidelines would not recommend adoption at the height of an emergency. As relief efforts shift from addressing immediate needs to reconstruction, the future and long-term care of children left orphaned after the tsunami remain in question. Although the Hague Convention legitimizes intercountry adoption as a means of providing a permanent family to a child "for whom a suitable family cannot be found in his or her State of origin," considerable debate about the role of intercountry adoption remains.

Opponents of intercountry adoption argue the practice exploits impoverished nations; robs children of the opportunity to be raised in their community of origin and identity; takes away resources that could be used to improve the lives of a larger number of children; and contributes to the problem of abduction, coercion and trafficking of children. Supporters of intercountry adoption counter that the practice benefits children by removing them from the detrimental effects of growing up in institutional settings or on the streets by providing permanent families; helps children who might otherwise be marginalized in their societies as a result of illegitimacy or racial/ethnic difference; and provides them with families in a context where there is little evidence that the elimination or restriction of intercountry adoptions would remove the problems of poverty that contribute to the abandonment of children.

The Hague Convention was created to address a large number of abuses that had come to light in the 1980s, by establishing a legal framework for the arrangement and formalization of intercountry adoptions. The Hague Convention deviates from the UN Declaration and CRC in that it sets out in the preamble a "hierarchy of options" believed to safeguard the long-term "best interests" of the child. These include preference for: 1) family solutions (return to birth family, foster care, adoption) rather than institutional placement; 2) permanent solutions (return to birth family, adoption) rather than provisional ones (institutional placement, foster care); and 3) national solutions (return to birth family, national adoption) rather than international ones (intercountry adoption).

Limitations of the Hague Convention

However, the Hague Convention only applies to countries that have ratified it and thereby are parties to it. As of 2004, only 46 countries had ratified the Hague Convention, including three of those hardest hit by the tsunami: India, Thailand and

Sri Lanka. Seven countries—including the United States, Russia and China—have signed but not yet ratified the Convention. In 2000, the U.S. Congress passed the Intercountry Adoption Act of 2000 (IAA), which authorizes the ratification of the Convention once U.S. preparations for its implementation have been established. Since that time, efforts have been under way to prepare and issue federal regulations for implementation so that the Hague Convention can be ratified, with finalization estimated for 2006. [The United States fully ratified the Hague Convention in 2008.]

With the exception of India and Thailand—which in 2004 sent 406 and 69 children, respectively, to the United States for adoption—intercountry adoptions from the tsunami-affected countries are rare. Sri Lanka and Indonesia permit the process, but are very strict about circumstances in which they allow it. Indonesia, for example, requires adoptive parents to live in the country for a minimum of two years and bars adoption of Muslim children by Christians. In addition, in accordance with Muslim practice, children who have lost both parents are expected to be raised by relatives, and if not relatives, then village residents or neighbors, and therefore would not be available for adoption. Despite the small number of intercountry adoptions, Indonesia and Sri Lanka responded to confirmed reports of child trafficking, recruitment of child soldiers, and Christian missionaries attempting to convert Muslim children by banning all adoptions.

Best Interests of the Child

Historically, the practice of intercountry adoption has been a humanitarian response to the plight of children in the aftermath of armed conflicts, political and economic crises, and social upheavals. The first intercountry adoptions occurred after the Second World War [1939–45]; subsequent groups of children—many born to Asian mothers and U.S. soldiers— were adopted at the end of the Korean and Vietnam Wars.

Economic crises and civil wars resulted in many children from Latin America being adopted in the 1970s and, with the fall of the Iron Curtain and massive media attention to the plight of children in such former Soviet states as Romania in the late 1980s, many children from central and eastern Europe were adopted overseas. Most recently, overpopulation in mainland China, a cultural preference for boys, and a "one-child" policy have contributed to the availability and adoption of thousands of abandoned Chinese girls overseas since the 1990s.

Notwithstanding the fact that the number of intercountry adoptions to the United States has nearly tripled since 1990, there appears to be a growing trend toward the restriction of intercountry adoptions. Romania enacted a law in 2004 that eliminated the practice (except for adoption by children's grandparents); and in January 2005 Russia passed a law that extends, from three to six months, the time orphans must be on the federal data bank before they are eligible for international adoption. The European Union [EU] is also requiring nations to "outlaw intercountry adoption as a condition for joining" the EU. South Korea introduced initiatives in March 2005, including a national adoption day, with the purpose of lowering the number of children sent abroad for adoption and of promoting domestic adoption. Consistent with these trends, most of the governments hardest hit by the tsunami have pledged to take care of the orphans within their own boundaries:

Indonesia. The government established several steps to protect children affected by the disaster. If reunification with parents or extended family is not successful, then children are to be placed in an orphanage, acquire foster parents or, as a last resort, be adopted. The Organisation of the Islamic Conference, the world's biggest grouping of Islamic nations, pledged $145 million to take care of the orphans, including through orphanages.

Sri Lanka. Legislation crafted with the assistance of UNICEF was introduced that would strengthen the existing system of out-of-home care by establishing provincial panels for the processing of foster care and adoption. The government has also invited a Texas-based Baptist agency, Children's Emergency Relief International, to develop foster care programs and the country's first child protective service.

India. The government has already pledged to provide the equivalent of $4,500 in aid for each child orphaned by the tsunami, half available immediately and the other half when the child turns 18. In addition, the government is considering new rules that would enable short-term foster care in the immediate aftermath of an emergency, thus minimizing the need for institutionalization.

Critics of this trend toward the restriction of intercountry adoption attribute its growth to the fact that many opponents are also involved in organizations that promote children's interests, such as international children's human rights organizations and UNICEF. These organizations tend to view intercountry adoption as subsidiary to both adoption and foster care within a child's country of origin.

Proponents of intercountry adoption argue that efforts to restrict intercountry adoptions tend to reflect political interests, and adversely affect children by extending the amount of time they will languish in an institution or remain on the streets. Based on research on the negative effects of early childhood deprivation, it seems clear that permanent solutions—including intercountry adoption—must take precedence over temporary solutions such as foster care or orphanages. Research in child development has shown that the quality of caregiver-infant relationships in the first years of life may be more important than the quantity of nourishment in facilitating healthy human development. Children who experience deprivation of a primary caregiver as a result of institutional care, or multiple caregivers in foster care, are at a greater risk for suffering from emotional, behavioral and developmental problems that impair their ability to form relationships, learn, and work in meaningful ways.

> *"Options for the orphaned children should be sensitive, kind, humane and, most important, child-centric, addressing the short- and long-term consequences. They have suffered enough."*

International Adoptions Exploit Tsunami Orphans and Result in Child Trafficking

Asha Krishnakumar

Asha Krishnakumar is an award-winning journalist for Frontline *magazine. In the following viewpoint, she reports on the struggle of organizations and governments to protect the vulnerable children orphaned by the December 2004 tsunami in Southeast Asia. Because of growing reports of child exploitation and trafficking by pedophiles, she explains, the prohibition against international adoption was a prudent way to deal with the problem.*

As you read, consider the following questions:

1. In Tamil Nadu, children made up what percentage of the tsunami casualties?

2. How many children were killed, orphaned, or made homeless by the tsunami?

3. According to UNICEF estimates, how many vulnerable children are victims of child trafficking by pedophiles every year?

Raji (10) and Ramesh (11) are happily playing among the heaps of clothes piled up near a relief camp in Nagapattinam, the coastal district in Tamil Nadu devastated by the tsunami. At first sight the orphaned children appear to have recovered well from the tragedy. But if one talks to them, their fears become apparent. They are petrified of water, of even going near the beach. "I am frightened of the sea," says Raji, holding onto Ramesh's hand firmly.

Children bore the brunt of the tsunami's wrath. According to the United Nations Children's Fund (UNICEF), children account for a third of the casualty. But in some districts of Tamil Nadu, the casualty was a staggering 50 to 60 per cent. Aid organisations talk of 1.5 million children dead, orphaned or made homeless in the disaster. Numbers apart, what makes the calamity poignant are the stories told by small coffins, children desperate for help and parents cradling the bodies of their infants.

Establishing Priorities for Tsunami Orphans

With thousands of children orphaned or separated from families, UNICEF has proposed a few priorities to save the "tsunami generation". They essentially involve ensuring the safety and health of the children, with an emphasis on clean water, adequate sanitation, basic nutrition and routine medical care. Separated children should be cared for, the agency said, adding that all relief plans must give high priority to finding children who have lost their families and reuniting them with their extended families.

It is especially tragic for the children who survived when their parents did not. In India, thousands of children have lost someone close to them—a parent, a sibling or a friend. For these children the tragedy is compounded by the lack of emotional support and by an uncertain future. For, the people they would turn to in case of a crisis are either dead or themselves grieving over the loss of kin and property. Such disasters also expose the lack, or the breakdown, of social systems that provide basic health, education and nutrition for children.

The vivid experience with destruction and death brings forth a wide range of responses and emotions from affected children. Reactions directly following the event are characterised as shock. According to paediatric psychiatrists, as the experience is so dramatic, extreme, sudden and even life-threatening, it is imprinted on the child's memory. This deeply embedded event is a disturbance that the child carries with him or her at all times. Long-term consequences include fear, vulnerability, depression, anger and sleep disorders, as well as repeated reliving of the event itself.

Twelve-year-old Arti, who survived the tsunami in Colachal in Tamil Nadu, hardly speaks since losing her cousin, and she "broods for hours", according to her mother, Helen Mary. Many parents have been complaining that their children are talking in their sleep. Eleven-year-old Mani, who was admitted to a hospital in Tamil Nadu's Thanjavur district, has not spoken a word for 10 days. According to child psychiatrists, a child, who has suffered from this traumatic experience, is particularly susceptible to the development of pathological symptoms.

Suffering Unimaginable Loss

UNICEF Executive Director Carol Bellamy said: "It is hard to imagine the fear, confusion and desperation of children who have seen enormous waves wash away their worlds and cast dead bodies upon the shore. Children have lost all semblance of the life they knew from parents, siblings and friends at home, school and neighbourhoods. They are in desperate need of care." UNICEF has begun to support government and local communities to assess the number and whereabouts of those who are separated from their families, or worse, their kin have not survived at all. With the aid of nongovernmental organisations (NGOs) and government authorities, it is developing systems to identify children and reunite them with their parents or other relatives.

District administrations in Tamil Nadu have ordered the enumeration of children living in relief camps without adult kin. Simultaneously, UNICEF is also counselling more than 100,000 traumatised children in the 13 affected districts. The organisation is collaborating with the State Social Welfare and Education Departments to implement the psychological care and support programmes.

The relief campaign, according to UNICEF, must help children cope with their trauma by getting them back to school as quickly as possible and by training adults, especially teachers and health workers, to interact with children to spot signs of trauma.

UNICEF has already trained several volunteers who have started working with children in Cuddalore. Training programmes involving an average of 120 volunteers per district will be held in the affected districts. This programme will be extended to the affected districts of Andhra Pradesh.

Government Efforts

As part of its effort, the Tamil Nadu government has decided to adopt all the children who have lost their parents. In a statement, Chief Minister [J.] Jayalalithaa said new homes to shelter at least 100 children each would be opened in Nagapattinam, Kanyakumari and Cuddalore, in addition to the already functioning government-run homes. She said:

The Tragedy of Human Trafficking

Every year one to two million women and children are trafficked across the globe, with the largest number—375,000—coming from the tsunami-battered shores of South and Southeast Asia. Lured by false promises of good jobs or simply kidnapped, trafficking victims soon find themselves chained to a life of forced labor, domestic servitude, illegal adoption or sexual exploitation.

Juliette Terzieff, "From Tragedy to Slavery,"
AlterNet, January 24, 2005. www.alternet.org.

"The opening of three new homes will ensure that no child is left in the lurch. Special provisions will be made especially for the kids. *Ayahs* [maids] will be appointed to take care of them. Playing materials and special medical facilities will also be part of such new homes."

The Government of India, according to Prime Minister Manmohan Singh, would provide education, sustenance and support for the affected children up to Class XII. Observing that special attention would be given to their rehabilitation and well-being, he said that government agencies had been asked to adopt the children and also assist NGOs in doing so.

The Issue of Adoption

There has been "overwhelming and outpouring" response from Indian corporate houses and individuals to provide assistance to the orphaned children as also in adopting many of them.

In this backdrop, asked if adoption laws will be diluted, Information and Broadcasting Secretary Navin Chawla said: "I think we will. . . ."

But this opens up a Pandora's box. Adoption may be one of the options, provided the safety and welfare of the child is ensured. There can be no dilution of the adoption rules as otherwise it would be risking the lives and well-being of the children. This is particularly important considering the large-scale nexus and trafficking in children that has been reported under the guise of adoption in the past. Evidence is also pouring in from all parts of tsunami-affected areas of child trafficking.

For instance, a UNICEF spokesperson, John Budd, told Reuters that a colleague in Kuala Lumpur had received an unsolicited mobile phone text message that offered to sell children "according to buyers' wishes". Read the message: "Three hundred orphans aged three to 10 years from Aceh for adoption. All paperwork will be taken care of. No fee. Please state age and sex of child required." Budd said: "If you read that text message, and if it is true, then either they have 300 orphans for sale or they have the capacity to seize children according to orders received."

The Indonesian government is investigating unconfirmed reports of child trafficking to Java and abroad. The government has banned Acehnese under 16 years of age from leaving the country. *Jakarta Post* reported cases of children being allegedly whisked away to Malaysia and the city of Bandung in West Java by an unnamed organisation in Medan. The *Guardian* of London quoted Carol Bellamy as saying that organised syndicates were exploiting the crisis in Aceh province. "Whether it is [for] adoption or exploitation purposes or sex trafficking, these are criminal elements. So it is very important not to let them get a foothold," she said.

Measures to Protect Tsunami Orphans

Concerned over such reports, Sri Lanka has banned the adoption of children affected by the tsunami until further notice. "Adopting the children until a permanent solution is implemented is illegal," a government spokesman told reporters after a Cabinet briefing. "Not even a Sri Lankan can adopt a child affected by this disaster until the government has come out with its programme," he said. "Even if they are relatives, they are not expected to take children without government permission."

In a televised interview from Rome, Pope John Paul II has asked the nations affected by the tsunami to be extremely careful about adoption as paedophiles around the world will take advantage of the situation and traffic orphaned children in large numbers.

Paedophiles love disasters, as social activist Mari Marcel Thekaekara wrote in her article in the *Hindu*. It gives them the golden opportunity to pick up abandoned children easily. Along with the burgeoning tourist traffic, India and Thailand are hot spots for paedophiles on the lookout for vulnerable children. According to paediatric psychiatrists, there is a clear pattern. They first befriend the kids in the guise of generous "uncles" and then, after winning their trust, inveigle the unsuspecting children into unsavoury sexual acts, which the children often do not even comprehend. UNICEF estimates that over 1.2 million children are trafficked every year this way.

What Is Best for Orphans?

Past experience shows that it is far better for the children to remain within the community. But, according to activists, attempts are already being made to 'arrange' adoptions. For a traumatised child to be taken away to a strange environment with different customs, languages, food habits and even possibly foreign parents would be extremely unsettling.

Around 60 child rights organisations have called for a yearlong ban on the adoption of children affected by the tsunami. They say this would prevent traffickers from exploiting children for cheap labour or the sex trade. It would also enable children to come to terms with their loss and allow time for counselling.

To assume that mere affluence provides a better life for a child is erroneous. Options for the orphaned children should be sensitive, kind, humane and, most important, child-centric, addressing the short- and long-term consequences. They have suffered enough.

Periodical Bibliography

The following articles have been selected to supplement the diverse views presented in this chapter.

Amy Anderson   "Experiences in Transnational Adoption: An Interview with Kim Park Nelson," Mamazine.com, February 4, 2006. www.mamazine.com.

Eve Conant   "The Battle over Tsunami Orphans," *Newsweek*, January 15, 2005. www.newsweek.com.

Gillian Flaccus   "Adoption Efforts Hampered," Associated Press, January 6, 2005.

Leslie Goldman   "An HIV Adoption Story," *Parenting*, December 2009.

Stephanie Holmes   "Saving Asia's Tsunami Orphans," BBC News, January 7, 2005. http://news.bbc.co.uk.

Ling Woo Liu   "Adopting Quake Orphans," China Blog, June 4, 2008. http://china.blogs.time.com.

Jim Luce   "First One Orphan, Then Many More," *New York Times*, November 12, 2007.

Melissa Jun Rowley   "International Adoption: A Good Deed When Done Right," Causecast, 2009. www.causecast.org.

Mike Sims   "Red Light for Tsunami Adoptions," CBS News, January 7, 2005. www.cbsnews.com.

Jane Jeong Trenka   "Transnational Adoption and the 'Financialization of Everything,'" *Conducive*, August–September 2009.

How Do Celebrity Adoptions Affect the Debate over International Adoptions?

Chapter Preface

In 2006, controversy erupted when Madonna, an internationally known singer, performer, and actress, filed papers to adopt a thirteen-month-old boy named David Banda in Malawi, Africa. Much of the controversy surrounded the perception of Madonna's manipulating the law to adopt David. Under Malawian law, prospective parents must normally wait eighteen months before finalizing the adoption process, but in Madonna's case, the judge gave her temporary custody during a two-week stay in the country. She was then allowed to fly back to England with him. This unleashed a firestorm of criticism from people all over the world who believed that Madonna leveraged her money and celebrity to circumvent the rules for her own gain. It also resulted in people questioning her motives, accusing her of ripping David away from his biological father and his African homeland for her own interests and quest for more publicity. It also led people to once again question the process of celebrity adoption and whether it was good for the larger practice of international adoption.

The country of Malawi is a small, impoverished country, with much of its population ravaged by AIDS. In fact, more than a million children have been orphaned by the disease, and the country does not have the resources to adequately deal with the influx of children, some of whom also are infected with the virus. In David Banda's case, he has a biological father who wasn't able to look after him. At two weeks old, David was placed in the Home of Hope orphanage, where Madonna found him.

Supporters of David Banda's adoption argued that he would have a better life with the pop singer. Financially, Madonna was able to provide a top-notch education and everything a child could ever want. Any physical or developmental issue could be dealt with by the best people in their fields.

And it was certainly better than growing up in an under-resourced orphanage, supporters contended.

Critics of the adoption countered that an African child should not be adopted by a foreign, white family. They viewed the adoption as a form of colonialism, with the privileged white woman coming in, manipulating the country's adoption laws, and taking away an African baby. Because she did get special treatment, Madonna was also accused of child trafficking. And when David Banda's father charged that he was not told the full truth about the process—that David would be taken away permanently—the charges of child trafficking raged even louder, with accusations of fraud and baby buying flying.

Madonna's adoption controversy echoes the issues that have always faced celebrity adoptions. More than non-celebrity families, the motives and tactics of celebrities are attacked—can these celebrities provide the attention and stability these children need? Are celebrities just following a trend set by superstars like Madonna or Angelina Jolie, and are these children just another fashionable accessory that will fall out of fashion next season? Or do celebrities have the same desires and motives that non-celebrity families have: loving homes they want to share with children who really need their help?

The viewpoints in this chapter review the controversial subject of celebrity adoptions and explore the impact they have had on the larger subject of international adoption. Topics discussed include whether celebrity adoptions are in the best interest of the child, if these adoptions are a form of colonialism and child trafficking, and whether they shine a much-needed light on the plight of orphaned or abandoned children.

> *"Celebrities are human beings just like all of us; being Angelina Jolie or Madonna does not make them more or less human."*

Celebrity Adoptions Are Helpful to the Practice of International Adoption

Selaelo Ramokgopa

Selaelo Ramokgopa is an accountant and a writer. In the following viewpoint, she asserts that celebrity adoptions are ultimately beneficial to the practice of international adoptions because they help children in need. Ramokgopa stresses that celebrities should have to go through the same adequate and appropriate processes that every prospective adoptive parent has to go through to adopt.

As you read, consider the following questions:

1. According to Ramokgopa, who should be blamed when adoption problems occur?

2. What problem occurred when Madonna adopted her child, David, from Malawi?

3. What responsibility does the celebrity have in the adoption process?

Adoption is a means by which people can alleviate or reduce the poverty that is affecting the world today. Would the world rather have one more child going to bed without food each night or can the world accept adoption as a way of avoiding a plight that is affecting millions of people over the world? Yes, adoptions including celebrity adoption do help international adoption relations. A celebrity adoption should not be viewed differently [from] any other adoption. Celebrities are human beings just like all of us; being [actress] Angelina Jolie or [entertainer] Madonna does not make them more or less human.

It will be hard to give the impression that adoption can have a negative effect on international adoption relations. As witnessed recently, there is a trend of celebrities adopting children from developing or third world countries. The standards of living in these countries are usually very poor and many families affected by poverty usually live on less than one United States dollar a day. These countries also seem to have a high number of orphans that they cannot afford to care for. To add to all these problems, adoptions by citizens of developing countries are usually not popular because the people are generally not well off economically. In many cases, authorities in countries where children are being adopted are usually happy with the fact that they will be spending on one less child and the adopted child will live in a loving environment. Adoptions, be it by celebrities or by ordinary people, will most likely strengthen or help international adoption relations.

Shady Adoption Practices at Fault

The issue that usually causes problems should be blamed purely on the adoption agencies or authorities in countries where the children are being adopted. What often comes to

Celebrities Shine a Light on Adoption

While experts don't attribute Africa's growing popularity among adoptive parents to a celebrity factor, they do say high-profile adoptions by the likes of Madonna and Angelina Jolie have raised awareness of the availability of orphans on the continent.

"One of the good things about the Madonna adoption or Angelina Jolie, those adoptions brought the need to the attention of Europeans or Americans," said Thomas DiFilipo, president of the Joint Council on International Children's Services. "And it brought the possibility (of adopting in Africa) to people's attention."

Celean Jacobson,
"Madonna's African Adoptions Part of Growing Trend,"
USA Today, *April 1, 2009.*

light after the adoption is the fact that the parents of the adopted children did not really agree on the adoption, that is, in cases where the children have biological parents. This is indeed a disturbing factor and an issue that the country where children are being adopted should deal with and try to address. There has to be proper, adequate and appropriate processes in place that need to be followed before a child can be adopted.

For example, when Madonna adopted her child, David, from Malawi, reports surfaced that the biological father of the adopted child did not really understand what adoption was. The father did not really understand that he will never see his little boy again. If true, that is a disturbing and sad fact indeed, and it is the duty of the authorities in the countries where the children are being adopted to ensure that the biological parents or guardians understand the process very well. The same issue also surfaced with Angelina Jolie's adoption of the little girl she adopted from Ethiopia, Zahara. Biological parents should be informed of the consequences of putting up a child for adoption and this responsibility should clearly be put on the shoulders of authorities in which the adoption occurs. When celebrities adopt, they sorely rely on the information being given to them by authorities in countries they are adopting [from], and it's fair to say that the reliance is justifiable given the fact that they do not live in the country.

Celebrities, like anyone else, need to ensure that they make use of reputable adoption agencies. This is an issue that should be handled with care and due diligence. Adoption, be it by a celebrity or any other person, is a good way of removing one child at a time away from poverty. International adoption is a way of improving relations between two countries while impacting the world positively.

> "Sure, celebrity adoptions have brought
> attention to Africa, but they could also
> lead to a dangerous bending of rules,
> one adoptive mother said."

Celebrity Adoptions Are Harmful to the Practice of International Adoption

Gabrielle Birkner

Gabrielle Birkner is a staff reporter for the New York Sun. *In the following viewpoint, Birkner examines the effects of the attention brought to international adoption by celebrities who adopt internationally, such as Madonna, who adopted a child from Malawi. While celebrity international adoptions have brought a lot of attention to the cause, some worry that the highly publicized rule bending by celebrities could lead to others circumventing adoption rules.*

As you read, consider the following questions:

1. How much has the international adoption rate increased since 1990?

2. What is a positive impact of Madonna's international adoption controversy?

3. Why could celebrity adoptions lead to a dangerous bending of adoption rules?

With Madonna taking to the airwaves to defend her decision to adopt an infant from a Malawi orphanage, more Americans could be inspired to consider African adoption.

Last year [2005], nearly 23,000 children born abroad were adopted into American families—more than three times the number of international adoptions in 1990. China is currently by far the most common go-to country for adoptive parents, with nearly 8,000 orphan visas granted from that country last year. Russia comes in a distant second, followed by Guatemala, South Korea, Ukraine, and Kazakhstan.

International Adoptions Increasing

But adoption counselors say would-be parents are increasingly turning an eye to African countries.

The number of Ethiopian and Liberian children adopted by American parents rose 66% and 94%, respectively, between fiscal years 2005 and 2006. During the 12-month period that ended in September, 731 children from Ethiopia and 353 children from Liberia were granted orphan visas, up from 440 and 182 the previous year, U.S. State Department figures show.

While the federal Office of Immigration Statistics does not provide a state-specific breakdown of adoptions by country, data show that New Yorkers go abroad to adopt in larger numbers than residents of any other state.

The president of the New York City chapter of the Adoptive Parents Committee, Samuel Pitkowsky, said adoptive parents who live in New York tend to be slightly older than their counterparts in other parts of the country. They are also more likely to be single, gay, and open to the idea of a multiethnic family, he said.

Copyright © 2006 Tab, the Calgary Sun, and PoliticalCartoons.com.

Celebrities Bring Attention to International Adoption

Stars such as Angelina Jolie, who took home an Ethiopian daughter last year, are spurring the rise in African adoption, according to the director of Americans for African Adoptions, Cheryl Carter-Shotts. She said news of Madonna's adoption of a 13-month-old could have a similar impact on would-be adoptive parents stateside. "The controversy wasn't good, but certainly it brought forward the need," Ms. Carter-Shotts said.

While adopting a child from China, Eastern Europe, or Latin America can cost $20,000 to $30,000—including agency, lawyer, and country-specific processing fees, in addition to paying for travel—adopting from Africa can be significantly cheaper.

Americans for African Adoptions charges adoption fees of $4,500 for children from Liberia and $7,500 from Ethiopia, not including travel. Ms. Carter-Shotts founded the agency shortly after adopting a teenage boy from Mali 21 years ago. She also has a grown daughter, whom she adopted from Ethiopia. In the past two decades, she has helped other Americans adopt some 600 African children. Most of these children were born in Ethiopia and Liberia, though the agency has placed youngsters from Mali, Sierra Leone, and Somalia in years past.

Critics have accused Madonna of bypassing Malawi's adoption laws, and even of kidnapping—claims that the singer denied in an interview that aired yesterday [November 1, 2006] on NBC. "I followed every rule, every law, and every regulation," she said. "All the criticism is ultimately a blessing in disguise, because now people know about Malawi, and about the orphans there."

Each year, Americans adopt about 130,000 children. That number comprises the international adoptions, some 15,000 domestic infant adoptions, and the tens of thousands of children who are adopted out of foster care or by a relative, according to the executive director of the Evan B. Donaldson Adoption Institute, Adam Pertman. The Boston-based Adoption Institute commissions research projects on adoption and advocates on behalf of adoptive parents and their children.

Mr. Pertman, the author of *Adoption Nation: How the Adoption Revolution Is Transforming America*, said African adoption is becoming increasingly common, amid the AIDS crisis there. "People see needy children, and they want to do something," he said. "The same thing happened in Romania after the fall of the Berlin Wall."

Could Celebrity Influence on International Adoption Be Dangerous?

Each country determines its processing fees and restrictions regarding the age and marital status of would-be adoptive parents. The amount of required paperwork and the average wait time also affect a country's popularity with those looking to adopt.

Sure, celebrity adoptions have brought attention to Africa, but they could also lead to dangerous bending of rules, one adoptive mother said. "What's to stop people with a lot of money for approaching the government to circumvent the rules and regulations in place to safeguard children?" Elise Stone, a Greenwich Village resident who with her husband, Craig Smith, adopted three children from Ethiopia, said.

The younger two children, Tesfahun, 9, and Hakima, 7, arrived five years ago, and Kerem, 11, joined the family last year. "People say, 'They're very American,'" Ms. Stone said. "I say, 'No, they're New Yorkers.' They stick out their hand to hail a cab, when they're tired of walking. They want to go out for Chinese food."

Ms. Stone, an actress, said that while many people prefer to adopt infants, taking in older children has its own rewards. "What we've enjoyed is watching the 'wow' factor as they've gone from living in a third world country to living in New York City," she said. "Never having seen a vacuum cleaner or Times Square—everything is a new and exciting experience."

> "A child in need of a loving home is a child, regardless of where on the planet she was born."

Celebrity International Adoptions Transcend Racial Barriers and Shed Light on Issue of Orphaned Children

Cindy Rodriguez

Cindy Rodriguez is a staff columnist for the Denver Post. *In the following viewpoint, she reflects on the vitriolic negative response to celebrities, such as Madonna and Angelina Jolie, who adopt babies from foreign countries, arguing that a lot of the negativity is rooted in discomfort with diversity. Celebrity international adoptions help to alleviate the stigma against interracial adoption.*

As you read, consider the following questions:

1. What is one of the main criticisms hurled at celebrities who adopt babies in foreign countries?

2. What does the author believe Angelina Jolie's three international adoptions have accomplished?

3. How does segregation impact one's attitude toward international adoptions, according to the author?

This season, yellow is the new black, patent leather shoes are a must, but—please!—"third world" babies are not a new accessory.

I've been disgusted by the response people continue to have about actress Angelina Jolie's international adoptions.

The star of the movie *Tomb Raider* is called "womb raider" on blogs. Tabloid-TV shows allow snarky critics to blather on about it being a quest for publicity. Even respectable newspapers have run stories quoting people who raise questions about her motives.

Two weeks ago, Jolie adopted a 3 1/2-year-old boy from Vietnam whom she named Pax Thien. He's her fourth child and I have no doubt she'll love him as her own.

Society Is Obsessed with Celebrities

While I don't usually concern myself with celebrity gossip, the rise of celebrity magazines and news programs—and the way such gossip has crept into the evening news—has made me think about the implications that celebrity adoptions have on the public.

In a Hollywood-crazed society, adoptions in Africa and Asia by stars such as Meg Ryan, Madonna, and Jolie are bound to have an effect on what people think of adoption, especially as it relates to adopting children of color.

It takes more than a handful of celebrities to create a trend. I have a hard time believing any of these women adopted for notoriety. Like Madonna needs media exposure.

Does Color Figure into Debate?

The topic is sensationalized partly because it centers on color. If these were children from poor European countries such as Russia or the Ukraine would there be as much hoopla? I doubt it.

Appreciating Diversity

There was a time when families who adopted children from a different ethnic or racial group were advised to cut ties to the past and assimilate the youngsters as completely as possible. Today adoption advocates agree that embracing the birth culture of these children is vital for parents raising kids from a race or culture other than their own. "When you raise a child of another race, you need to realize that you become an interracial family and to make use of every possible resource you can find to integrate with your child's birth culture," says Cheri Register, author of *"Are Those Kids Yours?" American Families with Children Adopted from Other Countries* (Free Press).

Amy Dickinson, "Bicultural Kids," Time, August 26, 2002.

Still, one of the main criticisms being hurled at these celebrities is they're adopting dark-skinned children because it's not "in" to get a white-skinned baby. They say those stars should take in American children.

I don't think we should get caught up in that sort of debate. A child in need of a loving home is a child, regardless of where on the planet she was born.

By becoming the mother of a Cambodian boy (Maddox), an Ethiopian girl (Zahara), and now Pax, Jolie is helping to diminish the stigma that's attached to children of color from poverty-stricken countries. It's helped call attention to the plight of 14 million orphans in Africa whose parents have died of AIDS.

United States Should Embrace Diversity

Any woman who adopts a child of another culture will have to deal with stares, stupid questions and with helping the child overcome feelings of cultural isolation. But these are not insurmountable problems and, frankly, it's a better life than remaining in an orphanage.

Really, it wouldn't be as big of an issue if the rest of us learned to feel comfortable with mixed-ethnicity families. (I refrain from using the term "race" because we're all from the same race: human.)

It's ironic that people living in one of the most diverse countries on the planet continue to struggle with diversity.

So many of us live segregated lives that impede our ability to understand each other.

The fortunate few live in diverse neighborhoods. The rest of us are wedged in enclaves of people who are just like us. (I'm no exception. In my neighborhood I can count on one hand the number of black, Latino and Asian faces I see. And it's rare to see anyone older than 70. My disclaimer: I had no idea it would be like this when I moved to LoDo [lower down-town area of Denver].)

Consequences of Segregated Lives

For some these separate-and-unequal lives are a choice; for others it's because they have no other choice. Income plays a huge role in determining where we can and can't live.

What we lose out on is the ability to connect with people of other cultures and to see the humanity of others who are different than us. Our comfort zones become a cocoon that serves as more of a trap than a sanctuary.

And it's from that disadvantage point that the critics judge those who dare go outside of their comfort zones. As long as it's a relationship of love, a white mom with a dark-skinned baby, or the reverse, is a beautiful thing.

"*[Madonna's] celebrity status allowed her to circumvent the country's strict adoption laws.*"

Celebrity International Adoptions Are Not in the Best Interest of the Child

Kate Sheehy

Kate Sheehy is a writer for the New York Post. *In the following viewpoint, Sheehy recounts the protests of more than sixty-five human rights groups over Madonna's recent adoption of a young Malawian boy. Critics claim that Madonna used her celebrity status to circumvent adoption laws. Critics also point out that the baby is not an orphan—his mother died in childbirth, but his father is alive and well. These experts argue that children should remain in their home country, taken care of by extended family or by their local communities.*

As you read, consider the following questions:

1. Why do human rights groups claim Madonna bought herself out of adoption requirements?

2. How did Madonna respond to claims that she did not adhere to adoption requirements?

3. What did the father of Madonna's adopted child say when asked about the controversy surrounding the adoption of his son?

It looks like Madonna is borderline adoption crazy—now she wants to take home a little Malawi girl, too.

A day after whisking a 13-month-old boy from the struggling African nation to her home in London, the superstar is already planning her next adoption—handpicking a 3-year-old girl from the same village where she found her soon-to-be new son.

"I looked at this child with questioning dark eyes and the saddest smile. I thought, 'She looks just like me,'" the 48-year-old singer and married mother of two gushed of the moment she spotted the little girl, according to London's *Daily Mail*. "I told [hubby] Guy [Ritchie], 'We must give this child a home, too.'"

Did Madonna Circumvent Adoption Law?

The singer's comments came amid international outcry over her sudden move to fly the boy out of his homeland Monday [October 16, 2006]—the same day that child advocacy groups had publicly said they planned to file a court injunction to try to at least delay his adoption.

The groups claim that Madonna—who has pledged to sink $3 million into dilapidated orphanages in the country—bought herself a way out of a key Malawi adoption requirement. Under the law, an adoptive parent must stay in the country with the child for 18 months so that social service workers can monitor the future family.

In a stinging response to her critics yesterday, the defensive diva issued a stunning statement, insisting that she and

Ritchie, a British director, "began the adoption process [of the boy] many months prior to our trip to Malawi" earlier this month.

"I did not wish to disclose my intentions to the world prior to the adoption happening, as this is a private family matter," Madonna said through her publicist, who released the letter.

"We have gone about the adoption procedure according to the law, like anyone else. . . . Reports to the contrary are totally inaccurate."

Penston Kilembe, the head of Malawi's Ministry of Gender, Child Welfare and Community Services, which oversees adoptions, backed the singer.

"The process did not start today—Madonna's people have been pushing papers for some time," Kilembe said.

But the singer's harshest critics, including more than 65 [human] rights groups, remained undaunted, flocking to court yesterday to protest her removing the toddler, David Banda, from the country.

They won the right to at least a hearing over whether her celebrity status allowed her to circumvent the country's strict adoption laws. It is likely to take place Friday.

Critics of Madonna's Adoption

There had been fear by the groups that the singer would try to move the baby—who has a temporary passport and visa—to her home in Los Angeles. Adoption rules in the United States are not as strict as in Britain.

But Madonna's flack last night said that while the singer would take the baby to the United States to visit family, she will raise him in London.

Justin Dzodzi, head of Malawi's Human Rights Consultative Committee, said the groups aren't opposed to the notion of Madonna with [the] adopted child. They just want her to adhere to the rules.

Steve Kelley Editorial Cartoon used with permission of Steve Kelley and Creators Syndicate.

"We want Madonna to stay here for 18 months and acquire residency as stipulated," he said.

He and others also complained that the baby is not an orphan. The boy's mother died soon after childbirth, but his struggling father, Yohane Banda, is alive and visited him when he could at the orphanage more than 25 miles from his home.

The father has given his blessing for the world's most famous female singer to take his child, after being assured she was a "good Christian lady."

Madonna is actually a follower of the Jewish mystical movement, Kabbalah.

Still, the dad yesterday asserted that foes of his child's adoption are simply "jealous of my son."

"What's their interest? I want David to have a bright future, not to live in this poverty," he said.

The singer sent an entourage of bodyguards and a personal-assistant nanny to gather the baby Monday. The group's whirlwind plane trip began on a private chartered jet from Malawi's capital of Lilongwe.

After a stopover in Johannesburg, South Africa, the entourage boarded a regular British Airways flight to London, where Madonna lives part-time with Ritchie, her 9-year-old daughter, Lourdes, and son, Rocco, 6.

A New Life

Aboard the aircraft, a passenger who sat next to the nanny and baby in first class noted that the boy already seemed to be reveling in his new life.

"The baby was happy and laughing and just so sweet," the woman, an American in her 30s, told the *Mail*. "He looks very healthy and is absolutely adorable."

The child was dressed in a white polo shirt, blue-jean shorts, red socks and brand-new sneakers. He also sported a tiny blue and orange baseball cap, making him sure to fit right in with his [brother] Rocco, who is frequently seen with ball caps.

As the toddler and his adult handlers left the plane at London's Heathrow Airport, the nanny tossed her sweatshirt over his head to shield him from photographers. He was then put in a Mercedes minivan and taken to Madonna's home in London.

The singer—crowing about the baby to relatives back in Michigan—said, "it's so worth it. He's just the best little baby ever!" according to *Hello!* magazine.

"Guy and I have never been happier."

> "If . . . you believe in adoption at all, it's
> difficult to draw the line and say that
> because of race or geography or culture
> one baby is an appropriate candidate
> for adoption and another is not."

Celebrity International Adoptions Help Children in Need

Carol Lloyd

Carol Lloyd is a writer for Salon.com. In the following viewpoint, she acknowledges the questionable history of white meddling in African countries, but argues that, at its root, celebrity adoption helps an impoverished child.

As you read, consider the following questions:

1. How many estimated orphaned children are there in Malawi?

2. Why did Malawian human rights organizations object to Madonna's adoption of a Malawian baby in 2006?

3. What did Romania do to their orphanage system?

Madonna's adoption opened a new international circus tent yesterday with the courts ruling in favor of 67 Malawian human rights organizations' application to help decide whether the middle-aged Material Girl and her filmmaker husband are fit to adopt David, the 1-year-old boy she met while visiting a Malawian orphanage and brought home with her to London.

Madonna's decision to mother a child from one of the world's poorest countries, where an estimated 1 million children out of a nation of 12 million have been orphaned, has evolved into one of those stories where everyone has an opinion—from Princeton's radical utilitarian philosopher Peter Singer to 8-year-olds in England.

The Controversy Regarding Celebrity Adoptions

The Malawian human rights organizations maintain that they are not against Madonna's adoption per se; they think the government didn't follow its own rules vis-à-vis Malawian laws that ban nonresident adoptions. But their objections to Madonna skirting due process have unleashed a larger controversy about the celebrity deus ex machina—rich white stars like Angelina Jolie swooping down to save poor dark children. This in turn has triggered a broader debate about all international adoptions. Is it ever right to whisk children away from their country and culture, instead of, say, giving their family (or some local family) the resources to raise the children in their native lands? Do international adoptions via orphanages inadvertently create baby markets where orphanage staff sell children and local parents are fooled into leaving their children only to have them disappear?

Objecting to the idea of Madonna with a stolen African child is understandable. The history of misguided do-gooding by the white, wealthy and powerful has such an intractable history that it's easy to just want to take the high ground and

Top 20 Primary Sending Countries in 2001

Country	Adoptions
China	4,723
Russia	4,279
S. Korea	1,870
Guatemala	1,609
Ukraine	1,246
Romania	782
Vietnam	737
Kazakhstan	672
India	543
Cambodia	407
Bulgaria	297
Colombia	266
Philippines	219
Haiti	192
Ethiopia	158
Poland	86
Thailand	74
Mexico	73
Jamaica	51
Liberia	51
Top 20 Total	**18,235**

TAKEN FROM: Evan B. Donaldson Adoption Institute, "International Adoption Facts," 2002. www.adoptioninstitute.org.

demand all charitable acts be vetted for selflessness. In some countries, orphanage systems have arguably done more harm than good. After the Romanian government closed its horrific orphanages, banned international adoption and created a foster care system and policies to keep children with their parents, the source of adoptable children also seemed to dry up. But in a place like Malawi, where there may not be enough healthy Malawian adults to adopt 1 million orphans, treating Madonna like she's a baby robber is ludicrous. It's asking that we preserve the culture of these malnourished, desperately poor orphans at all costs—even if it costs them their lives.

A Child in Need

No one disagrees that it would be better to work to alleviate the poverty that gives rise to orphanages around the world. Through her project Raising Malawi, Madonna is collaborating with the Millennium Promise, an organization seeking to end extreme poverty one village at a time.

I know I'll be slammed for this, but if you're not some sort of wacko lactivating comic mom and you believe in adoption at all, it's difficult to draw the line and say that because of race or geography or culture one baby is an appropriate candidate for adoption and another is not. I fear if all international adoption were banned there would be fewer people interested in the plight of these children. Besides, it's unreasonable to think that laws can transform the impulse to adopt a child into a desire for pure philanthropic action.

No matter what [writer and social critic] Caitlin Flanagan will tell you, mother love (or father love for that matter) isn't a wellspring of eternal goodness. It's an enlarging of our circle of selfishness to include someone else. But if that someone else is a child who might well have died, I can't help feeling that the act of adoption across borders offers a constant reminder that love and luck are terribly arbitrary. If other children could have been your own, why not take care of them too?

> "The thread that links all of these cases is that Africa is being used as a blank space on which these celebrities can project their own fantasies of 'saving' Africans."

Celebrity International Adoptions Are a Form of Colonialism

Adam Elkus

Adam Elkus is a writer and commentator. In the following viewpoint, he contends that the adoption of African babies by Western celebrities—particularly the Madonna case—smacks of colonialism in that it is reminiscent of Western powers coming in and abducting aboriginal babies to raise with Western values. In cases like this, Elkus argues, the baby is little more than a prop that is meant to show the celebrities' "chic internationalism" and make them feel like they did something to fight poverty.

As you read, consider the following questions:

1. How did Spanish, American, and Australian authorities justify the kidnapping of aboriginal children, according to to Elkus?

2. How did Madonna exercise "Western privilege" in her Malawian adoption?

3. How does the author believe that celebrities perceive Africa?

Celebrities have always identified with underdogs. Playing a victim or otherwise disadvantaged character is a sure route to an Oscar, and everyone from Bruce Springsteen to Eminem has celebrated the underdog in song. It's not surprising that models, actors, and popular musicians have focused on impoverished Africa, raising money and awareness for debt relief and famine. While admirable, these efforts have done relatively little to address the structural causes of African misery. There is also an uncomfortable element of colonialism that runs through celebrities' interactions with Africans and identification with African culture.

Is the celebrity fascination with Africa genuine or shallow? Are the efforts of well-meaning celebrities to liberate Africa from poverty and disease the continent's salvation or a recipe for disaster? Unfortunately, the answer is that the recent spate of celebrity adoptions, Angelina Jolie's much-hyped birth in Namibia, and Kate Moss's infamous blackface modeling in the *Independent* reveal cultural colonialism masquerading as liberal multiculturalism. And despite their good intentions, [Irish singer/songwriter] Bob Geldof and [vocalist for the band U2] Bono are being led around by the nose by technocrats and multinational corporations who bear responsibility for much of Africa's problems.

Madonna's Controversial Adoption

Madonna's "adoption" of a Malawian baby epitomizes the worst of the celebrity adoption trend. Malawi's stringent adoption laws force foreigners to stay 18 months in the country to be assessed as prospective parents. After concerted lobbying, a Malawian court issued an interim order allowing Madonna to take the child out of the country for a year, triggering court challenges from human rights groups and charities who felt Madonna had "bought" the ruling through her extravagant patronage of Malawian orphanages. Unwilling to wait, the pop singer deployed a team to spirit the child back to England. Madonna follows a celebrity trend started by Angelina Jolie, who adopted children from Cambodia and Ethiopia in deals of similarly dubious legality.

A naysayer might point out that the babies will lead better lives in the West. However, growing up in an alien culture separated from one's own ethnic traditions is a recipe for psychological problems. It has disturbing echoes of the Spanish, American, and Australian colonial practice of kidnapping aboriginal children in order to raise them with white Christian values; such kidnappings were justified by a similar desire to rescue the children from what was perceived as poverty both literal and spiritual. These issues are compounded by the objectification of celebrity adoptees by the media, which publicize them as exotic objects rather than human beings.

One also has to wonder about celebrities' real motivations. There certainly are plenty of babies of all races in their home countries who would benefit from their attentions. Why did these celebrities travel halfway around the world and go through a long and often frustrating process of international adoption? Was it because they wanted an "exotic" baby, appropriating a symbol of Africa to give literal weight to their oft-stated solidarity with the oppressed? There is no doubt that Madonna and Jolie love their children, but on a subconscious level, the babies are props that serve certain psychological needs. The babies demonstrate the celebrities' chic internationalism and make them feel like they have made a difference in the fight against poverty. For dilettante celebrities who believe they are serious crusaders against injustice, an "exotic" baby is an ego-boosting accessory akin to a Kabala red string bracelet, which similarly gives religious status to secular stars searching for "deep" meaning.

The Problem of Western Privilege

The most troubling aspect of the celebrity adoptions deal with elements of Western privilege, with Madonna and Angelina Jolie swooping into impoverished countries to essentially buy babies off families too poor to care for them. In Madonna's case, she technically abducted the baby, as her men took the baby before a Malawian court could rule against her. The most grotesque manifestation of colonial privilege occurred when Jolie turned a small corner of Namibia into an armed camp so she could give birth unmolested:

> Over the past six weeks a Western security force has effectively taken over the small African nation of Namibia. A beach resort in Langstrand in western Namibia has been sealed off with security cordons, and armed security personnel have been keeping both local residents and visiting foreigners at bay. A no-fly zone has been enforced over part of the country. The Westerners have also demanded that the Namibian government severely restrict the movement of journalists into and out of Namibia. The government agreed and, in a move described by one human rights organization as 'heavy-handed and brutal', banned certain reporters from crossing its borders.

Jolie essentially dictated security measures to a sovereign country, taking advantage of its poverty in order to have a "special" experience giving birth in Africa. She decided who entered and left the country, and carved out an exclusive space where she commanded a small army of private security officers. This favoritism is reminiscent of the behavior of colonial elites catalogued in Albert Memmi's classic text *The Colonizer and the Colonized*:

> If he is in trouble with the law, the police and even justice will be more lenient toward him. If he needs assistance from the government, it will not be difficult; red tape will be cut; a window will be reserved for him where there is a shorter line so he will have a shorter wait. Does he need a job? Must

he take an examination for it? Jobs and positions will be reserved for him in advance; the tests will be given in his language, causing disqualifying difficulties for the colonized. . . . From the time of his birth, he possesses a qualification independent of his personal merits or his actual class. He is part of the group of colonizers whose values are sovereign.

When one views the now familiar scene of a Western movie star and a television crew arriving to a god's welcome in a dusty African village, one cannot help but be reminded of the film *The Man Who Would Be King*, in which two British soldiers on the run are mistaken by Afghani villagers to be actual deities. Madonna and Angelina Jolie may have great respect for the orphans they advocate for, but their special treatment warps the power dynamics of the countries they visit. It is symbolic of a larger problem: Jolie is not the only Westerner with a private army allowed to operate as a sovereign force on foreign soil; oil and diamond companies maintain unaccountable private security forces in many impoverished regions.

Other Celebrity Controversies

While Jolie and Madonna's celebrity colonialism takes a physical form, Kate Moss's hits on a deeper level. In a high-tech update of the blackface vaudeville entertainers, Moss was digitally altered to look like a black woman for a special *Independent* issue on women in Africa. This is symbolic of the trendy celebrities' trendy Africanism. Moss can claim solidarity with African women and appropriate their identity via Photoshop, but at the end of the day she also can return to a safe home and a lucrative modeling career. Needless to say, the suffering women she identifies with cannot.

The devout Christian Bono is in many ways a modern version of the starry-eyed missionaries [who] went to Africa to save souls alongside the imperialists who strived for riches. Unlike his forbearers, Bono is not out to spread the cross, but its modern equivalent, liberal capitalism. He preaches from the stage about saving Africa's suffering masses while promoting economist Jeffrey Sachs, whose neoliberal "austerity" measures helped wreck Bolivia, Poland, and Russia's economies. As a consultant, Sachs mechanically applied orthodox free-market theories to radically restructure underdeveloped countries, exacerbating already formidable problems. This is the remedy Bono intends for Africa.

Sachs and his colleague Thomas Friedman are part of a group of centrist technocrats who live in a dream world where anyone, no matter how poor, can get out of poverty with a computer, and the solution to all development problems is opening markets. Bono also is a friend of President George W. Bush, whom Bono considers an ally in the fight for Africa.

Perhaps Bono might want to ask his friend George the next time they meet why the United States plans to spend $8 billion a month in Iraq when the five-year $3 billion U.S. AIDS contribution in 2003 will only be 14% of the total world AIDS expenditure in 2008?

While he's at it, perhaps he could get his pal Sachs to tell the International Monetary Fund [IMF] to stop making impoverished countries like Ghana double the price of water and electricity in return for a loan? If Bob Geldof was serious about reducing hunger in Africa, he would have tried to prevent the World Bank from forcing Mali to privatize its cotton sector. Then prices wouldn't have dropped 24% in one year in a desperately poor country where one in four people grow cotton for a living.

Providing Cover for Greedy Corporations

Instead of confronting the genuine causes of African poverty, Bob Geldof and Bono have allowed multinational corporations to continue to profit from African misery. While Geldof was putting on a show at Live 8 [a benefit concert], George Monbiot noted that the G8's [Group of Eight's] "primary instrument of US policy towards Africa," the African Growth and Opportunity Act, required African countries to bring about "a market-based economy that protects private property rights," "the elimination of barriers to United States trade and investment," and a favorable environment for United States foreign policy interests. In return African countries would receive "preferential treatment" for some of their products, *if* they use fabrics "wholly formed and cut in the United States" and avoid direct competition with American products.

It isn't surprising that this "preferential" treatment can be terminated if it "results in a surge in imports" or that implementation of the agreement has been contracted to a lobby group representing Halliburton, ExxonMobil, Coca-Cola, General Motors, Starbucks, Raytheon, Microsoft, Boeing, Citigroup, and other multinational corporations. Desperately poor countries will break their backs trying to privatize while the United States and Europe keep their massive subsidies.

The thread that links all of these cases is that Africa is being used as a blank space on which these celebrities can project their own fantasies of "saving" Africans. For celebrities like Bob Geldof and Bono, Africa is also a vehicle for a grand moral struggle. As Brendan O'Neill of *Spiked* writes,

> This brand of moral grandstanding suggests that Africa has become a kind of plaything for some campaigners, a backdrop against which they can make themselves feel good and 'special'. They are searching for personal meaning and purpose in the deserts and grasslands of Africa, not kick-starting a meaningful debate about how to take Africa forward.

History Repeats Itself

There is little new about this. The 19th-century missionaries and explorers who established European control over the continent saw it as an exotic and forbidding land in which a similar kind of personal meaning could be found (or lost). The actual thoughts and desires of the inhabitants mattered little.

Madonna on Malawi

Visiting Malawi can be a very humbling experience. In the face of such overwhelming challenges, it's easy to feel helpless. At the same time, it is impossible not to recognize how much we can do to improve the lives of vulnerable children.

Madonna, "Will You Join Me?" Huffington Post, *October 28, 2009. www.huffingtonpost.com.*

Celebrities see Africa in a similar way. Jolie, Madonna, and Moss have convinced themselves that they have some kind of connection to the suffering African masses, despite their immense wealth and fame, and they search for public ways of proving that connection. They confuse this wish fulfillment and fetishization of the exotic for meaningful measures that are actually helping Africans. Similarly, Bono and Geldof may think they are reducing human misery, when they are really just preaching the gospel of free-market wealth to suffering Africans. That's the most obscene part about the celebrity crusade for Africa: Jolie and Madonna's antics take public attention off the continent's real problems, and do-gooders like Bono and Geldof give rhetorical cover to those who bear responsibility for a substantial portion of those problems.

When it comes down to it, colonialism is still colonialism, even if it poses in a fashion magazine, plays a *Tomb Raider* in the multiplex, or strums a guitar. One cannot ascribe malicious motives to the celebrities—they sincerely believe they are making a positive difference. But they are not. While celebrities "find themselves" in Africa's plains, the IMF, World Bank, and multinational corporations are out to find profit.

Periodical Bibliography

The following articles have been selected to supplement the diverse views presented in this chapter.

Yasmin Alibhai-Brown	"My Friend Tindy Proves Celebrity Adoptions Can Be Inspirational," *Daily Mail* (London), July 23, 2009.
Alexis Fitts	"Madonna vs. Malawi, Part Two," *Mother Jones*, March 31, 2009.
Steven Gaines	"Hungry Heart," *New York*, April 10, 2009.
Donna Goodison	"Celebs Take Lead in Adoptions; Stars Put Focus on Overseas Children," *Boston Herald*, October 23, 2006.
Celean Jacobson	"Debate Rages over Ethics of Celebrity Adoptions in Africa," *Toronto Star*, April 2, 2009.
Kay Johnson	"The Tale of Angelina's New Son," *Time*, March 22, 2007.
Thomas Mountain	"What Did Angelina Jolie Pay for Her Baby?" *CounterPunch*, December 30, 2009.
Emily Nussbaum	"The Nuclear Family, Exploded," *New York*, August 13, 2007.
Raphael Tenthani	"Madonna Wins 3-Year-Old 'Mercy' from Malawi," *USA Today*, June 12, 2009.

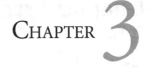

CHAPTER 3

What Are the Consequences of International Adoptions?

Chapter Preface

One of the biggest concerns about international adoption is the challenges and obstacles the adopted children face once they are legally adopted and brought to their new home countries. Being taken from one culture and placed in another is obviously a tricky issue for well-adjusted children, never mind those with sometimes serious physical, developmental, or emotional problems. When these children are faced with prejudice from those around them in their new homes, such challenges become even more difficult.

Critics of international adoption maintain that placing a child from a different country into an American home can result in discrimination against the child and the family. Many Americans, these critics charge, will not be accepting of families composed of different races or ethnicities and, as a result, the child will suffer from discriminatory attitudes all through his or her life. As a result, he or she may feel alienated from his or her adopted heritage as well as his or her native heritage and feel that he or she doesn't fit in anywhere. Some adopted children have reported feeling this way, and these perceptions have profoundly affected their lives and well-being.

Supporters of international adoption counter by asserting that America is changing; moreover, the way Americans perceive the idea of family is evolving. Whereas once families composed of different races or ethnicities would be very rare, today they are much less so. In addition, many resources exist to help adoptive families and adopted children transition and thrive, such as cultural education programs for adopted children to learn about their country of origin; post-adoption counseling; and classes for adoptive parents to educate themselves on how to help their children face discrimination and keep their children connected to their own cultural identity.

The challenges for families and children are numerous, but supporters of international adoption argue that loving families that educate themselves and prepare themselves for these risks can meet such challenges. With both sides looking for the best option for children, the debate will continue.

The following chapter presents viewpoints that discuss many of the main challenges adoptive families and children must face once they are settled in their new homes. Some of the subjects explored are the discrimination against adopted children, the fear that the child will be alienated from his or her cultural heritage or suffer from developmental delays, or that international adoption will encourage child trafficking. On the other hand, the beneficial consequences of international adoption are also examined, such as providing for children with disabilities, addressing discriminatory policies put in place by foreign governments, or ultimately facilitating the evolution of American society into a more tolerant, color-blind community that respects people of all races and nationalities.

> "Transracial adoption is unique and by embracing racial diversity and preparing for poss ible issues, [an] adoptive family can ensure their child has [a] positive racial identity and strong self-esteem."

International Adoptions Break Down Racial and Ethnic Stereotypes

Angela Krueger

Angela Krueger is a writer focusing on issues of adoption and parenting. In the following viewpoint, she asserts that being a multiracial adoptive family can be a rewarding experience if the family chooses to provide their adopted child with a racially diverse home environment that can develop racial awareness for the whole family.

As you read, consider the following questions:

1. Why is transracial adoption controversial, according to the author?

2. What are some ways adoptive parents can create a racially diverse home environment?

3. How can prospective adoptive parents prepare for the challenging experience of adopting a baby of a different race or ethnicity?

Most prevalent among Caucasian families, the process of transracial adoption has been met with controversy. Some people feel that children should be adopted by a family where one parent shares the child's ethnicity to promote positive racial identity and self-esteem.

Others believe that the love for a child is what matters most and the child's race should not play a role in the selection of an adoptive family. Regardless of whether prospective adoptive parents are adopting domestically or internationally, there are some major considerations that need to be addressed before making the decision to adopt transracially.

Why Transracial Adoption Is Good for Families

Being a multirace adoptive family can be a culturally rich experience if the family chooses to embrace their diversity and seek out opportunities to expand their cultural horizons. By creating a racially diverse home environment with books, movies, artwork and music representing the child's race, adoptive families help instill a positive identity for the child and also develop racial awareness for the whole family.

Transracial adoptive families also have the opportunity to broaden their social network by connecting with people sharing the child's race through friendships and professional relationships they might not otherwise experience. Adoptive parents need to look for racial diversity when choosing:

- Health professionals

- Hairdressers

- Babysitters

- Youth groups

Changing American Families

Americans adopted 7,044 Chinese children last year [2004], the U.S. State Department reports. Nearly 16,000 more came from other countries, including Korea, Russia, Nepal, Guatemala and Ethiopia.

Such adoptions are literally changing the face of some American families and challenging racial and cultural stereotypes along the way.

"When a child comes home, family members are forced to deal with preconceived notions about race on the most intimate level," says Jennifer Dole Massie, regional adoption supervisor for Lifelink [International Adoption]. "It does a huge amount of good in terms of race-relation building."

Michael Braga,
"Changing Face of Some Families Often Means
Big Adjustments for All," Sarasota Herald Tribune,
May 22, 2005.

- Churches
- Day care providers
- Shopping centres and grocery stores
- Restaurants and entertainment

Transracially adopted kids also benefit from cultural festivals and activities where they can blend in and give adoptive parents the experience of being a visible minority.

Challenges of Adopting Transracially

As a transracial adoptive family, everything is outwardly focused and family members need to come to terms with being noticeable in the community. Here are some common issues multirace adoptive families need to prepare for.

- People often assume that the child was adopted internationally and will direct their questions as such.

- It is necessary to discuss racial prejudice and racism as a family to help adopted kids deal with concerns.

- Strangers may ask intrusive questions about hair care and the child's ability to speak English in derogatory ways.

- Others may stereotype that an adopted child would be highly athletic, academically strong or musically inclined because of [his or her] race.

- Adoptive parents need to be on constant alert to correct negative perceptions of the child's birth family or birth country.

- It may be necessary to move to a more culturally diverse neighbourhood so the child has a positive sense of self and can be surrounded by role models of many races.

Living as a transracial adoptive family can be challenging at times but there are also many positive things about being a multicultural family. The key to making racial diversity a good thing for adopted children and their families is to ensure everyone involved feels comfortable talking about race and understands possible issues before they arise.

Preparing for a Transracial Adoption

Considering what life as a multicultural adoptive family might be like before choosing to adopt a child of a different race is a good exercise for prospective adoptive parents. In addition to reading books and articles on transracial adoption, it may be helpful to do a course such as one offered by Adoption Learning Partners and to listen to interviews by adoption experts.

It is important that prospective adoptive parents understand that lacking prejudice is not enough when it comes to adopting a child of a different race. Transracial adoption is unique and by embracing racial diversity and preparing for possible issues, [an] adoptive family can ensure their child has [a] positive racial identity and strong self-esteem.

> "I was abandoned, sold, white-washed and later disowned. My white mentality, my white words and my white memories betray the reality of my brown skin."

International Adoptions Result in Discrimination

Mateo Cruz

Mateo Cruz has dedicated the last eight years to working with and learning from young people of color. He works at HIFY (Health Initiatives for Youth) developing a team of peer health educators in East Oakland, California. In the following viewpoint, Cruz excoriates the practice of international adoption. Born in Colombia and adopted by a white family in Montana, Cruz suffered from racial discrimination throughout his life and struggles with an ongoing crisis of identity.

As you read, consider the following questions:

1. What does Cruz know about his young life in Colombia?

2. How does Cruz describe growing up as a brown-skinned Latino in Montana?

3. What is an example of some of the racism Cruz describes experiencing as a child?

I am a Colombian man. I do not speak Spanish. I cannot dance. And, I am in love with a white woman.

I was born in 1979 at an unknown place to an unknown woman in Bogota, Colombia. What is known is that on March 10, I was placed in a basket on the steps of a run-down orphanage and legally determined abandoned. The nuns guessed that I was about 6 weeks old. That is what I know about my life in Colombia.

Raised Away from Home

Six months later, a young Christian couple from Bismarck, North Dakota, paid $5,000 to adopt me, after seeing my picture in their local church's missionary newsletter. This was their third time to adopt from the agency: They were already raising one little girl. The second child died before they could bring her home. My adoptive mother's devastation gave her a hidden determination to save me, at all costs.

My mother is now in her 50s. She's a white woman in small-town Montana. She has always been strikingly beautiful and young-looking, often being misread as my older sister. People often said that she was the kindest woman they had ever met. She was the model Christian wife, hardworking and dedicated solely to her family. She worked 60 hours every week and gave all she had and then some to her family, hoping that her children would live the life she only dreamed of.

My father was one of the most openly racist people in my life. He was raised in an abusive home in North Carolina and became the product of his misogynistic, homophobic and racist upbringing. He was the one who told me that if it wasn't for him, I'd be picking coffee beans on a plantation. He cheated on my mom openly until they divorced when I was 5, leaving her with two kids and a mortgage. At night, she would crawl into my bed and cry. She would talk to me for hours and hold me tight and say, "I love you so much. Promise me you won't ever change," I promised, and she told me that I was her very best friend, her only friend in the world.

Rarely did we ever speak of Colombia or adoption growing up. My mom had a lot of fears—the fear that someone was going to come take me away, the fear that I would want to return to Colombia and look for my birth mother and the fear that my father might kidnap me in the night. Those fears kept me from ever exploring my past or my history because I refused to do anything that would hurt her.

Racial Discrimination

Growing up as a brown-skinned Latino in Montana was not easy. Most of the kids read me as Native American and treated me with such disdain. When I was in third grade, they called me a "chocolate-covered raisin," among other things. I fought on the playground daily for my right to exist. I earned respect, yet remained a target.

My mother tried to protect me the best way she knew how, by not acknowledging my brown-skinned reality. She would hug me and tell me, "Don't worry, honey. You are beautiful. It's like you have a year-round tan!" She would tell me how beautiful she always thought brown babies were, with their dark eyes and dark hair. I think I was her lifeline to another world, one more exotic and exciting than her real life.

Later in my childhood, my mom married a man who was already raising two daughters. We became one of the newest trends in the United States: the blended family. Although my mom fought with my sisters often, she and I never had conflict. In fact, the first fight we ever got into was over my hair. I was 19 years old, and I had returned from college with bleached blonde hair. She was so angry, but all I could understand her saying was that she just wanted babies with dark hair. That night, I stayed at my grandma's house. While she

Adopted Children by Place of Birth and Region: 2000

Nativity and place of birth	Total		Northeast		Midwest		South		West	
	Number	Percent	Number	Percent	Number	Percent	Number	Percent	Number	Percent
Total	1,586,004	(X)	284,242	(X)	389,096	(X)	548,297	(X)	364,369	(X)
Native	1,386,868	(X)	231,135	(X)	339,805	(X)	498,962	(X)	316,966	(X)
Foreign born[1]	199,136	100.0	53,107	100.0	49,291	100.0	49,335	100.0	47,403	100.0
Europe[2]	36,800	18.5	9,946	18.7	9,412	19.1	11,300	22.9	6,142	13.0
Russia	19,631	9.9	5,109	9.6	5,376	10.9	6,355	12.9	2,791	5.9
Romania	6,183	3.1	1,414	2.7	1,653	3.4	1,788	3.6	1,328	2.8
Ukraine	2,328	1.2	673	1.3	568	1.2	630	1.3	457	1.0
Asia[2]	98,368	49.4	26,454	49.8	28,200	57.2	19,419	39.4	24,295	51.3
China	21,053	10.6	6,718	12.6	4,399	8.9	4,682	9.5	5,254	11.1
India	7,793	3.9	2,056	3.9	2,383	4.8	1,258	2.5	2,096	4.4
Korea	47,555	23.9	13,047	24.6	17,330	35.2	8,134	16.5	9,044	19.1
Philippines	6,286	3.2	1,124	2.1	1,213	2.5	1,564	3.2	2,385	5.0
Vietnam	4,291	2.2	1,055	2.0	763	1.5	1,201	2.4	1,272	2.7

continued

Adopted Children by Place of Birth and Region: 2000 [CONTINUED]

Nativity and place of birth	Total		Northeast		Midwest		South		West	
	Number	Percent	Number	Percent	Number	Percent	Number	Percent	Number	Percent
Africa	3,111	1.6	790	1.5	640	1.3	996	2.0	685	1.4
Latin America[2]	58,166	29.2	15,595	29.4	10,553	21.4	16,730	33.9	15,288	32.3
Central America[2]	32,476	16.3	4,791	9.0	5,455	11.1	9,455	19.2	12,775	26.9
Guatemala	7,357	3.7	2,106	4.0	2,097	4.3	1,647	3.3	1,507	3.2
Mexico	18,201	9.1	903	1.7	2,168	4.4	5,242	10.6	9,888	20.9
El Salvador	2,254	1.1	722	1.4	252	0.5	758	1.5	522	1.1
South America[2]	20,354	10.2	8,029	15.1	4,776	9.7	5,318	10.8	2,231	4.7
Colombia	7,054	3.5	3,318	6.2	1,636	3.3	1,507	3.1	593	1.3
Northern America	1,576	0.8	270	0.5	277	0.6	607	1.2	422	0.9

X - Not applicable
[1]Foreign born includes 1,115 children born in Oceania who are not shown separately.
[2]Includes areas not shown separately.

TAKEN FROM: *Adoption Factbook IV*, National Council for Adoption, 2007.

did apologize, she made the same request of me that she had always made: just don't ever change.

Conflict in the Home

For the next three years we fought. She hated that I identified as a person of color. She would scream, "What does that mean? White is a color, too!" After three years of fighting, I explained to her that I could not be who she wanted me to be, and I could not have her in my life if she could not accept me for who I was. I left it for her to decide to accept me as I am or close the door forever. I have not seen, heard or spoken to her since.

I am now 27 years old and live in Oakland, California. I moved here five years ago to try to find a connection to political communities of color. But, I ended up still feeling like an outsider. I could not relate to their experiences or histories. All I knew was my own reality, one where my closest friends and family members were all white. I tried dating women of color, but there always seemed to be that same disconnect. Soon, I fell in love with a white woman, one who was full of the kindness and love that reminded me of my mother.

When my girlfriend and I used to walk by groups of people of color, I longed for their acceptance. As we edged closer, I imagined their words for me: sell-out, white-washed, traitor, I would feel ashamed. I conceptualized their words for who she might be to them: racial fetishist, trophy wife, stupid white girl. I would feel sad and torn. I imagined them shaking their heads thinking, "Damn, we lost another good man of color, stolen from us by some stupid white woman."

The last thought is more accurate than they know. I was stolen, I was abandoned, sold, white-washed and later disowned. My white mentally, my white words and my white memories betray the reality of my brown skin. But not because my white girlfriend made me this way.

Between Different Worlds

There is a unique complexity for anyone living between identities, between different worlds. We are aliens: Our existence is both suspect and intimate. We know that nothing is black or white, good or evil. Each of our stories is different and folded in the complexity of love and hatred, fear and safety, newness and loss, and privilege and racism. That privilege is now both my savior and my captor.

At night, the same dreams haunt me. They are always about war, violence, whales beneath the water, the ocean and my mother. I think in the end, they are all about my mothers, both of them. I have one mother who gave me away and one who gave me up, and I loved them both, with everything in my being.

> "The adoption of children by parents of another racial or national background illustrates both the fluidity and tenacity of racial and ethnic boundaries."

International Adoptions Illustrate the Fluidity of Racial and Ethnic Boundaries in American Society

Hiromi Ishizawa, Catherine T. Kenney, Kazuyo Kubo, and Gillian Stevens

Hiromi Ishizawa, Catherine T. Kenney, Kazuyo Kubo, and Gillian Stevens are professors at the University of Illinois at Urbana-Champaign. In the following viewpoint, they chronicle the changing U.S. attitudes toward international interracial adoption. The authors investigate the growing tolerance toward and acceptance of blended, interracial families by both individuals and society, concluding that these attitudes are conditioned by one's personal experiences with issues of race and ethnicity.

Hiromi Ishizawa, Catherine T. Kenney, Kazuyo Kubo, and Gillian Stevens, "Constructing Interracial Families Through Intercountry Adoption," *Social Science Quarterly*, vol. 87, December 2006. Copyright © 2006 Southwestern Social Science Association. Reproduced by permission of Blackwell Publishers.

As you read, consider the following questions:

1. According to the authors, how many visas per year was the United States granting by the turn of the twenty-first century for children adopted overseas?

2. How many foreign-born children under the age of eighteen were living in the United States in 2000?

3. According to a study by the U.S. Department of Health and Human Services, what percentage of white women would adopt a child of another race?

The number of children from abroad who have been adopted by Americans has increased dramatically over the last decade. In the early 1990s, the number of children born abroad and adopted by U.S. parents vacillated between 7,000 and 9,000 each year, but by the turn of the 21st century, the United States was granting almost 20,000 visas per year allowing Americans to adopt children ranging in age from infancy to early adolescence from more than 100 different countries around the globe, although three-quarters of the children were from just six countries (China, Russia, South Korea, Guatemala, Ukraine, and Romania). By 2000, there were almost 200,000 foreign-born adopted children under the age of 18 living in the United States.

The rise in intercountry adoptions has sparked discussion in several different disciplines. There are rapidly growing literatures, for example, investigating the health and welfare of the adopted children. A number of studies document demographic, social, and political reasons for the rise in the demand for adoptive children from abroad and for increases in the supply of children born abroad who are available for adoption. Other scholars discuss the issues of social justice, the role of nation-states, and international legalities involved in intercountry adoption.

Role of Race and Ethnicity in International Adoption

In this [viewpoint], we investigate the role of race and ethnicity in intercountry adoption in the construction of American families.... [We] begin with the premise that adoption is a site in which the culture at large works out its understanding about "family," including the issue of who can be integrated into a family. We also argue that parents who construct interracial families by adopting children of different national and racial origins illustrate the fluidity and tenacity of racial boundaries in a manner akin to adults who form interracial families by marrying across racial or ethnic lines. However, no study to our knowledge has investigated the patterns of adoption among the rapidly growing number of U.S. families with one or more children adopted from abroad. Therefore, in this [viewpoint], we seek to answer the following three questions.

1. Do American parents adopt children of their own racial and ethnic background? For example, are Asian-American parents most likely to adopt children from an Asian country? Are white American parents most likely to adopt children from a European country?

2. Does the probability of adopting a child whose race matches the race of the parents vary according to the attributes of the adopting family? For example, does the presence of other children in the household matter?

3. Does the probability of adopting a child whose race matches the race of the parents vary by the other characteristics of the child? For example, parents may prefer to adopt children of a particular sex, or a particular age, and consider the child's race of secondary importance.

The above questions are analyzed using descriptive statistics and, for white American parents, a multinomial logistic regression model predicting the race of a child adopted from abroad. The data are from the 2000 U.S. Census, which is the first U.S. Census to have asked whether children in a household were the biological children, adopted children, or stepchildren of the householder.

The Racial Composition of American Families

The default norm governing the racial composition of American families has been racial homogeneity. The norm of racial homogeneity within families has been expressed in laws and expectations concerning the match between the race, ethnicity, and national origins of children and their adopting parents. The expectation of racial homogeneity in American families was historically most stridently expressed in state-level anti-miscegenation laws, which were struck down by the Supreme Court only in 1967. Until the 1960s, interracial adoption was illegal in many states—with the "acceptable exception" of the adoption of Asian children from abroad by (non-Asian) American citizens after World War II, the Korean conflict, and the Vietnam War.

Over the past 50 years, policy debates regarding interracial adoption—within the United States, as well as in sending countries and in international bodies attempting to regulate intercountry adoption—have reflected complex and often conflicting understandings of the interests and rights of adopting parents, adopted children, nation-states, and variously defined racial, ethnic, or nationality groups. Attitudes and policies in the United States have shifted several times over this period as a result of these conflicting understandings and of variation in the influence of different groups. For example, the first domestic "transracial" project, which was enacted by the Child Welfare League of America and the Bureau of Indian Affairs in 1958, specifically promoted the adoption of American-Indian children by non-Indian parents. However, as the numbers of Indian children adopted by white parents grew, concerns grew that removing Indian children from the tribes would harm the stability of Indian families. As a result, the Indian Child Welfare Act of 1978 allows the adoption of Native American children by non–Native American parents only under very special circumstances. Similarly, in the context of the political and social climate of the civil rights movement, in the 1950s and 1960s organizations such as "Parents to Adopt Minority Youngsters" actively promoted placement of black children in white families. However, many adoption agencies geared their services away from interracial placement after the National Association of Black Social Workers termed interracial adoption a form of "race and cultural genocide" in the early 1970s. The organization still offers a strongly worded statement about their preference for black children to be placed with black parents. At the same time, the passage of laws such as the Refugee Relief Act of 1953, designed to allow American parents to adopt war orphans from Korea, meant that the most common source of transracial adoption over this period was intercountry adoption.

The Shifting Debate

Over the 1980s and early 1990s, the domestic debate over transracial adoptions shifted again, due to concerns that agencies' racial-matching policies contributed to delays in the adoption of children of color, leaving a disproportionate number of these children to languish for long periods in foster care or institutional settings. In response to these concerns, Congress passed the Multiethnic Placement Act of 1994 (MEPA), later amended by the Interethnic Adoption Provisions of [the Small Business Job Protection Act of] 1996, which prohibits an agency or entity that receives federal assistance from delaying or denying the placement of a child on the basis of race, color, or national origin of the adoptive or foster parent or of the child. (However, the Interethnic Adop-

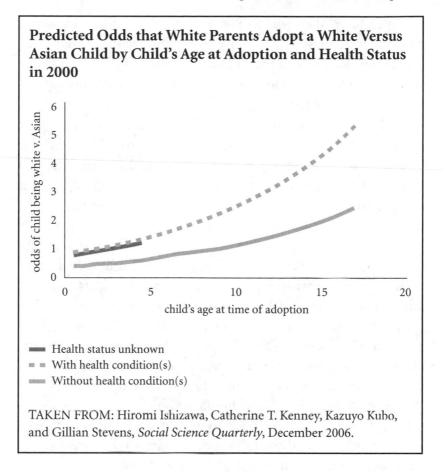

Predicted Odds that White Parents Adopt a White Versus Asian Child by Child's Age at Adoption and Health Status in 2000

odds of child being white v. Asian

child's age at time of adoption

━━ Health status unknown
▪ ▪ With health condition(s)
━━ Without health condition(s)

TAKEN FROM: Hiromi Ishizawa, Catherine T. Kenney, Kazuyo Kubo, and Gillian Stevens, *Social Science Quarterly*, December 2006.

tion Provisions of 1996 specifically state that the amendment does not apply to placement of Indian children.)

The largely color-blind stance of MEPA contrasts with growing concerns raised internationally about the merits of adoption across national and cultural boundaries. For example, the 1993 Hague Convention on Protection of Children and Co-operation in Respect of Intercountry Adoption suggests that intercountry adoption should be the last resort and that priority should instead be given to enabling children to remain with their [families] of origin or be adopted within their [countries] of origin. Similarly, the United Nations Convention on the Rights of the Child contains language guaranteeing children the right to personal, familial, communal, and national identities. These conventions thus assume that children, even if infants at the time of adoption, already have specific cultural origins and that it is in a child's best interests to maintain those origins.

Similar views regarding a preference for children to be raised within their "birth culture," as well as the interests of a nation-state in preventing the loss of its children, are reflected in policies enacted in recent years by a number of individual sending countries. [Barbara] Yngvesson stresses the significant role played by sending countries in determining which children are "adoptable." Sending-country policies also regulate which parents are acceptable as adopters, including such considerations as parents' race, age, and marital status. For example, Ukraine has instituted a waiting period of one year before an intercountry adoption is allowed in order to first exhaust the possibilities for within-country placement (although exceptions are allowed in the case of children who suffer from a disease listed with the Ministry of Public Health Protection); Kenyan law prohibits adoptions by parents of a different race than the child except under "extenuating circumstances"; South Korea's guidelines give preference to parents who have been married for at least three years and who are between 25 and 44 years old; and several countries, such as Paraguay and Romania, have adopted laws entirely banning intercountry adoptions by nonrelatives. Such sending-country policies reflect varied and evolving ideologies about the rights and identities of children, and they also affect the composition by race, age, and health status of children who are available for adoption by U.S. parents.

Facts About International Adoption

Currently, little is known about the characteristics of adopted children and their adopting families in the United States. Early in the 1990s, [Kathy] Stolley concluded that the 1987 National

Health Interview Survey (NHIS) provided the most recent data describing the incidence of interracial adoptive families. In that survey, 92 percent of all adoptions involved same-race adoption and of these, 85 percent involved a white mother adopting white children. However, a study on adoption by the U.S. Department of Health and Human Services showed that although over 50 percent of white women indicated that they would prefer to adopt a white child, almost 90 percent would accept a child of another race. This apparent change in the parents' preferences concerning the race of children that they would consider for adoption may be embedded in the series of changes in federal laws as well as in international policies concerning adoption.

Whether the race or ethnicity of adopted children from abroad "matches" those of their American adoptive parents is thus an important question for numerous reasons. One set of issues concerns the needs and rights of children, as set forth in the United Nations Convention on the Rights of the Child, to maintain the culturally distinctive understandings and behaviors of their origins. Another concerns the discourses within families and communities of "belonging" and of the (im)mutability of racial and national-origin characteristics and racial and national memberships. Intercountry adoption thus generates serious questions about the determination of racial and cultural boundaries and human rights; when overlaid with interracial or interethnic adoption within the destination country, the questions become even sharper.

International Adoptions and Interracial Marriage

The questions raised by interracial adoption also include issues of racial and ethnic boundaries within families and within the larger American context. In some ways, adoption across racial lines parallels interracial marriage. Both result in the formation of interracial families. Both are predicated on an important familial relationship, whether parent-child or husband-wife, in which the default expectation is that the family members match on race. But there are differences. Interracial marriages presume that both partners agreed to participate in an interracial relationship, but interracial adoption presumes that only the parent(s) agreed. Interracial marriages often provide a site blending two family lines, while in the case of interracial adoption the adopted child typically arrives without known background family ties. In addition, while interracial couples involve adults with differing racially specific upbringing and socialization, adopted children, especially when adopted early in life, are socialized in their family of upbringing and so opportunities for the clashing of culturally specific expectations are minimal.

A major difference between interracial adoption and interracial marriage rests on the ability of only one party to the decision—the adopting parents—to explicitly weigh the importance of health status, race, sex, and age in constructing their family. The availability of children with some constellations of characteristics (e.g., healthy or white or infants at the time of adoption) is, however, limited relative to the demand. American parents may therefore trade one desired characteristic of the child for another. For example, if prospective parents weigh the age of a child at the time of adoption more heavily than the child's race, they may prefer to adopt an infant of a different race than to adopt an older child of the same race as themselves. Parents who already have a child or children and wish to "balance" the children in their family by sex may weigh the sex of an adopted child more strongly than the child's race or age.

The Changing Face of American Families

The adoption of children by parents of another racial or national background illustrates both the fluidity and tenacity of racial and ethnic boundaries. On the one hand, the melding of people of different origins into one familial unit serves to blur racial boundaries for those living within the household and others with intimate ties to the household. If the child is very, young when adopted, the adoption may erase the very notion of cultural difference at the individual level unless the parents overtly attempt to cater to their child's background, which [Carl A.] Kallgren and [Pamela J.] Caudill argue happens only rarely. In a more recent ethnographic study of U.S.-China transnational adoption, [Sara K.] Dorow frames adoptive parents' approach to cultural practices in four different ways—*assimilation, celebrating plurality, balancing act* (of two cultures), and *immersion* (into a minority culture). On the other hand, the decision by prospective parents to adopt a child of a different race is most likely conditioned by their ideology of race in America and their personal experiences and understandings of it. This means that the prospective parents' perceptions of the meaning of race may result in varying distributions of children by race among adoptive families depending on what race(s) parents consider acceptable among members of their family.

We therefore argue that prospective parents consider race or ethnicity, among other attributes such as age, sex, and health status, when deciding to adopt a child from abroad and to raise the child as their own in the United States. Unlike parents deciding to bear a child biologically, adoptive parents have choices with respect to the racial and national origins of their child—although these choices are constrained to some extent by the availability of children of selected origins and the relative difficulty or ease of adopting children with certain characteristics from specific countries. For example, the vast majority of children available for adoption from China are girls. The race of adopted children, when considered within the context of the parents' own race, will thus illustrate the relative importance of race and national origins as criteria for family membership.

| *"When people talk about the adoption, they don't care about how the child grows up or how it affects the birth mothers."*

International Adoptions Alienate Children from Cultural Heritage

Kim Young-gyo

Kim Young-gyo is a writer for Yonhap News Agency. In the following viewpoint, Kim reports on a movement of Korean women and Korean adoptees who oppose South Korea's adoption system, which has sent thousands of orphaned and abandoned children abroad. These parents and children feel that South Korean children adopted by foreign families are alienated from their cultural heritage.

As you read, consider the following questions:

1. How many domestic adoptions of Korean children have occurred since 1953?

2. How many international adoptions of Korean children have occurred since 1953?

Kim Young-gyo, "Korean Adoptees from Abroad and Birth Mothers Protest Overseas Adoption," Yonhap News Agency, August 5, 2007. Copyright © 2007 Yonhap News Agency. All rights reserved. Reproduced by permission.

3. Where does South Korea rank on the list of countries that send children to the United States for adoption?

Roh Myung-ja has gotten together with her son every year since 2004, when she was reunited with him after giving him up for adoption about 30 years ago. She is one of thousands of Korean women whose children were adopted overseas.

The 49-year-old Roh believes what she has experienced in the years before her son returned to her should not happen to anyone. Now, she works as a staff member of Mindeulae, (Dandelions), a civic group of South Korean parents whose children were adopted overseas and who oppose the nation's adoption system, which sends thousands of orphaned and abandoned children abroad.

"We hope that no other mothers have to go through the pain and suffering that we went through. Overseas adoption leaves deep-rooted scars both on the birth mothers and the children," Roh said in an interview with Yonhap News Agency on Saturday [August 4, 2007].

A Movement to End International Adoption

About 30 Korean adoptees from abroad and 10 birth mothers, including Roh, came together Saturday for a rally in downtown Seoul calling for the government to abolish international adoption from South Korea. The mothers and adoptees were not all related to each other.

They held up picket signs that read, "Real Choices for Korean Women and Children," "Korean Babies Not for Export" and "End Overseas Adoption."

A signature-gathering drive also began to express opposition to overseas adoption. The civic group plans to collect one million signatures nationwide.

Government figures show that there have been about 87,500 domestic adoptions, versus 158,000 international adoptions, since the end of the Korean War in 1953.

A Personal Story

In 1977, Roh had to give up her 11-month-old child, and had no idea that her son had gone to the United States.

"I was literally shocked when I got a phone call in 2004 saying that my son is coming from the U.S. to look for me," Roh said.

Roh said that no one asks or is responsible for what happens to the children after they were adopted overseas.

"My son luckily turned out fine. But who knows what other kids undergo?" she said. "The day when I took my son shopping for the first time, he said to me, 'This is my first time in my life that I went shopping without caring that I am not white.'"

Roh's son, who was not able to make a trip this week to Seoul from South Dakota, wholeheartedly supports her actions, she said.

Keep Child's Interests in Mind

Jae Ran Kim was one of the adoptees from overseas who joined in Saturday's protest. A social worker focusing on domestic adoption in the U.S., Kim was adopted from South Korea by a U.S. family in 1971.

"When people talk about the adoption, they don't care about how the child grows up or how it affects the birth mothers," she said. "The adoption system is too much dominated by the adoptive families and the adoptive agencies."

Kim stressed that she did not have [a] negative experience as a Korean adoptee in the U.S. and is in a good relationship with her adoptive parents.

"It is not a matter of whether you had a good experience or bad experience as an adoptee. The adoption system goes way beyond that. It works within a political, institutional structure of society," she said.

Evolving Concepts of Cultural Identity

The understanding of the importance of cultural identity is still evolving says Virginia Appel, executive director of Adoption Alliance in Denver, which currently places children from Guatemala, Colombia, Russia and Bulgaria.

"We have come so far in international adoption in the last 30 or 40 years," she says. "I don't think it was considered unimportant before, but what was considered of primary importance was finding loving homes for these children and getting them out of orphanages."

Today it is more of a two-pronged approach: Providing good homes remains the highest priority, but the obligation no longer ends there. Appel says parents must make an effort to educate themselves about their children's homelands and heritages.

Jenny Deam,
"'Why Not Take All of Me?' Advocates Worry That the
Culture of Origins Left Behind in International Adoptions,"
Denver Post, *September 1, 2002.*

Adoptees Lose Their Cultural Heritage

Kim, who was on her third visit to South Korea, has not been able to find her birth parents yet, but plans to live in South Korea with her husband and children for a while in the future.

"Adoption does not only affect me as an adoptee, but it also affects my family—my husband and children. My children do not have their grandparents in South Korea, and they lost their part of the Korean culture, too," she said.

She argued that a child should be adopted by the extended family or extended community at least, and that international adoption should be the last option.

South Korea, the world's 11th-largest economy, was the fourth country in 2004 following China, Russia and Guatemala to send the most children to the U.S. for adoption, according to a research paper by Peter Selman, a British scholar.

> "Unlike in years past, when children brought to this country were expected to meld in with the dominant culture, today's adoptive parents are told ... that they need to 'do culture' for their children."

International Adoptions Do Not Necessarily Alienate Children from Cultural Heritage

Martha Nichols

Martha Nichols is a freelance writer and editor. In the following viewpoint, Nichols describes her own struggles to help her adopted child stay connected with his cultural heritage and explores the trend of "culture keeping," which refers to the practice of adoptive parents providing educational and cultural activities for their adoptive children to help them learn about and engage with their native cultures.

As you read, consider the following questions:

1. In 2008, the number of immigrant orphan visas dropped by what percentage since 2004?

2. How many foreign children have been adopted by U.S. families in the past twenty years?

3. According to the author, what is the danger of pushing a child's birth culture on them too hard?

This past March, my son Nicholas Hiep missed a week of first grade. He had a fever that shot up and down but never quit, and so his pediatrician sent him to get a chest X-ray. Nick was cheerful, throwing kung fu punches in the halls of Mount Auburn Hospital; I was cranky, missing more work.

Nicholas turned to me with a wicked grin. *"Me oi!"*

That's "Hey, Mom!" in Vietnamese.

A white woman sitting nearby gaped at me—I'm tall, blue-eyed, Julie Andrews in a scruffy leather jacket—then Nick.

"Is this the hospital where they called me Noojin?" he asked.

"No," I said. "That was Children's."

"Why did they say Noojin?"

Nick knew this story, so it wasn't a matter of verifying the facts. When he was a baby, he'd had swollen lymph nodes under one armpit, probably a reaction to the TB vaccine he received in Vietnam. Soon after returning to the United States, we took him to Children's Hospital in Boston. At that time, his health-insurance card was still under his Vietnamese surname: Nguyen. The physician's assistants always called out "Noojin."

"Lots of Americans don't know how to say Nguyen," I whispered.

"But you do. We do."

"That's because we learned."

For an English speaker, "win" approximates Nguyen, one of the most common yet elusive of Vietnamese names. Maybe Nick thinks we've cracked a secret code. He told me recently that Nguyen Thanh Hiep is his true name.

At these moments, I'm sure my husband Rob and I are doing something right. Like many international-adoptive parents, we work hard to incorporate our son's birth culture into our lives. For years, we've followed the formula for what's sometimes called "culture keeping": celebrating the main holidays from Nick's birth culture; buying ethnic artwork, clothing, or food; spending time with other international adoptive families, perhaps going to a "culture camp" for a few days each summer.

Some would say I take it to extremes. I enrolled in a Vietnamese language class the year before Nick's adoption in 2002. Last fall, I signed up for another course that meets five days a week. At the same time, I found a Vietnamese tutor for Nick.

In December, Rob and I took Nick on a trip to Vietnam, his first visit back to his birth country. But just weeks before we left, we found ourselves with a child melting down, who was terrified we'd leave him there, afraid we'd be disappointed if he didn't like it. "I don't want to go to Vietnam!" he howled. "I don't want to go to Vietnam! I . . . don't . . . want . . . to . . . go . . . to Vi-et-*nam*!"

It was then that I thought maybe I'd gone too far. Was I doing this more for myself than for Nick? I know the caveats. He was too young; it's normal for a first grader to be contrary. All true, and he often infuriated me in Vietnam. I was proud when he told people his name in Vietnamese, but I never felt at ease. We were on public display more than in any American hospital hallway. I worried for my boy when saleswomen fussed over the long rattail in his hair, fingering it, saying he was "lucky." I kept wanting to hug his tense little face against my chest.

Since our trip, I've talked to people inside the adoption community and out: other parents, adoptees, social scientists, Vietnamese Americans. Going overboard can be worse than doing nothing at all, so I wonder and fret: How much should I push cultural activities onto my son? How much of his birth culture is it healthy for him to keep as he grows—and how much is confusing or harmful, a kitschy pastiche that will leave him permanently unmoored?

In 1999, close to four hundred Korean adult adoptees met in Washington, D.C., at a three-day event known as The Gathering. A research study, published the following year by the Evan B. Donaldson Adoption Institute, a nonprofit advocacy organization based in New York, surveyed 167 Gathering participants about their sense of identity. More than a third said they had identified as Caucasians growing up—until they figured out they weren't.

"I felt different and alienated and alone," goes one typical quote from the study. Another said, "[I was a] freak—I tried not to think about it."

In recent years, the push to standardize culture keeping has been spurred in large part by flak from this older generation of international adoptees. Unlike in years past, when children brought to this country were expected to meld in with the dominant culture, today's adoptive parents are told very explicitly by adoption agencies that they need to "do culture" for their children.

A few decades ago, international adoption was about humanitarian aid—period. The granddaddy of agencies, Holt International in Eugene, Oregon, got its start in 1956 with Harry and Bertha Holt's Christian fervor to help Korean war orphans. In the mid-'70s, children endangered by the aftermath of the Vietnam War made their way to America through Operation Babylift. The press, churches, and nonprofits involved all trumpeted adoptive parents as noble do-gooders.

Today the philanthropic line alone doesn't cut it. It's considered harmful to adoptees, who rightfully don't want to grow up feeling grateful for food and shelter in the U.S. Many adult adoptees have begun speaking out about the racism their white parents didn't acknowledge and the loss of birth families and culture.

Take this quote from a 2009 survey by the Adoption Institute of five hundred adult adoptees: "Going to Korea changed my perception. . . . When I returned home, I loathed white people. I grieved the loss of being around others who looked like me and I took it out on the white people around me." That's enough to pour cold water on any adoptive parent's dream of a smooth and harmonious blending of cultures.

Many adoptees express raw anger, especially when they're young adults. Others come to terms and even celebrate their dual identities. In both cases, however, the internal conflict is clear. Hollee McGinnis—aka Lee Hwa Yeong—a Korean adoptee in her thirties, says she had a lot of pride in her heritage as a child, "but it shriveled right up when someone called me a 'chink.'" Her adoptive family was always supportive, she's quick to add, but she grew up in a "Caucasian" town north of New York City.

She describes one emblematic trip to a Korean restaurant when she was twelve. Her parents and older siblings were the only whites in the place; nobody else was speaking English. McGinnis says her family looked at her "as if suddenly I'm going to remember everything about Korean food and know what to order. It was just funny being placed in this situation, feeling very awkward, very uncomfortable, but also enjoying *kimchee*."

McGinnis, director of policy and operations at the Adoption Institute and lead author of the 2009 study, is married to another Korean adoptee. Together, they have a one-year-old son. She laughs when talking about her son's white grandparents and how confusing it must seem to him.

Plenty of McGinnis's peers are less amused by such tales. In memoirs, on Facebook, and in Yahoo! groups, adult transracial adoptees often hit back at adoptive parents (or "APs") who won't listen to their pain. Yet as McGinnis points out, we only hear from the ones who care about losing their birth cultures. "There's a group of adoptees that don't care squat," she says. "The vast majority of adoptees are doing the dance—putting on Asian culture, taking it off, figuring it all out."

The crucial factor for adoptees seems to be whether their adoptive parents ignored their racial difference when they were children. A number of adoptee memoirs describe birth-parent reunions and cultural reconnections, but these writers—like McGinnis, who reunited with her birth family in 1996—didn't all start the identity quest feeling traumatized. White parents who told kids that "color doesn't matter" or "that woman who abandoned you is *not* your real mother!" were probably denying a whole lot else about their children—a tip-off that bad parenting was the culprit, not a lack of culture keeping.

Meanwhile, the media chatter on about international adoption when, in reality, it's in sharp decline. In 2008, the immigrant orphan visas processed by the State Department had dropped by twenty-four percent since the peak in 2004. Most adoption experts believe the downward slide will continue. China is releasing far fewer children for adoption, and the waiting period for prospective parents can be over three years. Vietnam, Cambodia, Guatemala, and several other countries are now closed to U.S. adoptions.

Yet international adoptive families take up far more space in the zeitgeist than is warranted by actual numbers. The sum of U.S. international adoptions over the past twenty years comes to about 300,000 children. That's in a country of 300 million people. Not chump change, but also not the "explosion" often cited by journalists or social scientists.

Nick is growing up American, and during our trip to Vietnam he clung to that like a barnacle. But as the months have gone by, I can see he absorbed something while there of Vietnam, too. He is both; he is neither.

In a photo from our trip, Nick crouches on one knee at the edge of Hoan Kiem Lake in downtown Hanoi. His hands are crossed in another kung fu move. He's not exactly smiling. He wears a long-sleeved striped shirt and dirty running shoes, which don't identify him as American, but his pose does—his direct gaze at the camera, his back to the gray lake and misty sky and ruined Tháp Rùa—the Turtle Tower.

Then again, his gaze may be what my boy brought into the world. When I first saw baby Hiep, cradled in a nanny's arms at five months, he stared right back at me. I'd expected him to avoid eye contact, to be scared of the hulking white people. I thought he'd cry or shriek. Instead he just stared with his big dark eyes, and I knew he was mine.

What you don't see in the picture of Nick and placid Hoan Kiem are the lanes of screeching motor scooters around the lakefront park. That ethereal mist in Hanoi? An inversion layer of pollution. Nick crouches alone, without us, without any of the Vietnamese who daily use the park for *tai chi* or badminton or idling. I wonder what he'll think when he looks at this photo as an adult. Will he condemn us? Will he remember how he howled, "I don't want to go to Vietnam!"? Will he understand how uncomfortable we all felt?

There's now an ocean of information available about how to "bring culture home," to paraphrase a recent *Adoptive Families* magazine article. Starting in the early 1990s, when countries like China, Russia, and Vietnam required adoptive parents to travel overseas to meet their children, the focus of adoption literature has shifted to celebrating the birth cultures of adoptees.

Families with Children from China (FCC), which began with a few adoptive families in New York City and Seattle, now lists parent-support groups in all fifty states and in other countries. And since 2000, many more culture camps have sprung up from coast to coast. At these camps, adopted children of specific heritages spend a few days together making paper dragon heads, learning a bit of Chinese or Kazakh, performing in talent contests. Often the whole adoptive family participates in a sleep-away weekend.

Catalyst Foundation, a humanitarian· organization in Northfield, Minnesota, opened its first Vietnamese culture camp in 2001. Thirty-four Minnesota families attended. Now Catalyst runs an East Coast camp as well. Executive Director Caroline Nguyen Ticarro-Parker says attendance at both camps has shot up, averaging eighty to one hundred adoptive families at each location.

Our family went to a Catalyst camp north of Boston in 2007. We still wear the green T-shirts with stylized dragonflies and "VIETNAM" in block letters. I loved watching crowds of lean brown children running around the cafeteria or dodging actual fireflies outside. But I also remember sitting in an auditorium with all those kids and their white, gray-haired parents, feeling disconnected. A few days of educational fun didn't seem like enough.

Ticarro-Parker says that eighty percent of the families who attend Catalyst camps think going there once a year constitutes culture keeping. Like many other Vietnamese Americans in their early forties, Ticarro-Parker left Vietnam right before the fall of Saigon in 1975. She's the adoptive mother of twin eleven-year-old daughters from Vietnam, and her husband is white. For culture keeping to be real, she says, "it has to be a part of your life every day—it can't just be an event."

But some adoptive parents still assume that their children will be untouched by racism because they're growing up in a white household. At the Catalyst camps, parents now get their own sessions about racism. Yet at one of the first, Ticarro-Parker reports, "we had parents walk out, [saying] 'this will never happen to my child!'" Why not? "'Because my child's white.'" Ticarro-Parker snapped right back: "'No, she's Vietnamese!'"

At its most superficial, celebrating birth cultures has spawned a mini-industry of stuff to be bought—jeweled red threads and ladybugs, adoption-day cards, child-size Vietnamese *ao dai* (traditional fitted robes and pants), *non* (conical hats)—all available at the camps or online. In Ho Chi Minh City in December, I shopped in the tourist stores along tony Dong Khoi street, ticking down my list of gifts for friends back home, allowing Nick to buy a paper snake on a string, a Year of the Snake T-shirt. It felt like a forced march to consume rather than a means to forging cultural connections.

"I have seen more families bring home cartloads of items from where they went," says Elizabeth Vergo, a social worker in her early seventies who conducted our pre-adoption home study seven years ago. Before she retired from MAPS Worldwide, our adoption agency in Boston, she was director of adoption training.

"I think Chinese-adoption people do too much—because it's available, every town has a Chinatown—it's sort of simple," she adds. "I know families who are ten years home and still having Chinese New Year's together. Did anybody ever ask those children [what they wanted]?"

McGinnis of the Adoption Institute puts it this way: "Now I worry that we expect the girl adopted from China will be interested in all things Chinese. How much are we pushing the racial stereotypes onto our kids?"

For many Americans, other countries are cool, of course. It's fun to buy a green coconut to drink from a sidewalk vendor in Saigon, to climb Mayan pyramids, to flirt with new traditions like the Lunar New Year. God knows, I'm not immune. But often our desire to explore "amazing" developing countries around the globe is self-serving. The heritage we white parents chase doesn't have much to do with Asian Americans, for example, or the big buzzing conundrum of contemporary China and Vietnam.

When sociologist Heather Jacobson talked with China-adoptive families in the Boston area in 2002, many reported making trips to Chinatown in search of "authentic" immigrants rather than connecting with assimilated Chinese Americans. In a recent phone interview, she said some of these mothers said, "I want the real thing."

In her 2008 book *Culture Keeping: White Mothers, International Adoption, and the Negotiation of Family Difference*, Jacobson analyzes research she conducted with forty China- and Russia-adoptive families around the same time Nick came home with us. Families adopting from China in the 1990s saw themselves as "pioneers," she says. But since then, Jacobson has observed "solidification" of culture keeping. Newer adoptive parents have an attitude that seems to say, "'It's kind of all set up for me, and I don't have to make any decisions about it—I can access it when I want to and not.'"

Jacobson, herself the mother of a four-year-old daughter, sees culture keeping as part of today's intensive-parenting juggernaut. Many middle-class adoptive parents, overworked and overly invested in their kids, feel relief that "there's this ready-made avenue to do culture," she says. "'Here's the way you can do it, it will be fun!'"

But feeling relief that you don't have to think about it gives me pause. Jacobson and other observers point out that white parents often celebrate a child's birth culture in lieu of dealing with a child's race. They want a formula, not daily dissonance.

While some harried adoptive parents grab for Culture Lite, others leap way overboard. Culture keeping often carries the whiff of the helicopter: Little Lily has to be in a lion-dance troupe and be trilingual by the age of ten *and* play the piano, or else—what? She won't get into Harvard. She won't be happy.

The problem with pushing anything on kids, be it music lessons or birth culture, is that they may end up hating what's good for them. Many adult international adoptees say they wish their adoptive parents had pushed them to learn their birth language, for instance. Not knowing Korean or Vietnamese makes it harder to communicate with birth parents, or to get beyond the tourist gloss. It's a mantra I've taken to heart. Yet healthy separation may mean it's better for adopted children to do such learning on their own. Many adult Asian adoptees report diving into identity quests when they first leave home for college, with their white parents no longer hovering. The other problem is that culture keeping for many adoptive families is also cultural *creation*. Beyond the simplistic—strewing your house with red lanterns—it can turn bizarrely convoluted, as adoptive parents struggle to both affirm a strange land and deny its problems. In the past ten years, a steady stream of social scientists like Jacobson has been studying international adoptive families, particularly through interviews in the China-adoptive community. What they reflect back is rarely flattering.

Take this circa-2001 story:

> For my daughter's baby-naming we hybridized something from a baby boy's thirtieth-day celebration that we saw in a Zhang Yimou movie: Villagers passed the baby through a giant, donut-shaped, decorated steamed bun, so we had a bakery make us a giant donut-shaped challah and passed her through at the end of the naming ceremony to much delight and applause.

Crazy parent or lovingly involved? The story appears in anthropologist Toby Alice Volkman's *Cultures of Transnational Adoption*, a 2005 essay collection she edited. Volkman got the donut-challah pass from a Yahoo! group contact. Volkman is not a disinterested observer; she and her husband adopted a daughter from China in 1994. But like any good feminist social scientist, she's fascinated by how families construct themselves. You could call the challah pass creative, but when white families make up the cultural rules, there's an element of self-righteousness, too, as well as acquisitiveness. Americans pick and choose their ethnic affinities according to personal taste.

Others would argue that international adoptive parents aren't as wacky as they used to be. "In the beginning there was a tremendous sense of adventure," says Susan Caughman, editor in chief and publisher of *Adoptive Families*. Her peers "were very in love with Chinese culture and thought about keeping it alive for their children. No one saw that it would become quite the phenomenon it became."

Caughman and her husband adopted their now seventeen-year-old daughter from China in 1991. Caughman was a founder of one of the first FCC groups in New York. With her daughter presently looking at colleges, she has come to think of culture keeping as something that happens in developmental stages and which can't be forced. "Once they're eight or nine, it's kind of over with you managing it," she notes.

> "It's an emotional issue that goes to the heart of what people are seeking when they adopt a child—and the obstacles they can face in this country."

International Adoptions Neglect U.S. Children in Need

Jocelyn Noveck

Jocelyn Noveck is a journalist. In the following viewpoint, she explores the reasons behind why so many children are adopted from foreign countries when there are so many American children waiting for permanent placement while in foster care. Noveck acknowledges that the domestic adoption process is long and arduous and often frustrates willing adoptive parents.

As you read, consider the following questions:

1. How many children are currently in the U.S. foster care system, waiting to be adopted?

2. How many children do Americans adopt from overseas every year?

3. In 2005, how many children were adopted by American families from China?

Jocelyn Noveck, "As International Adoptions Rise, Some Wonder Whether U.S. Kids in Foster System Are Forgotten," AP Worldstream, October 26, 2006. Reprinted with permission of the Associated Press.

Angelina Jolie adopted from Cambodia and Ethiopia. Madonna, as most of the planet knows, is adopting from Malawi. And ordinary Americans adopt foreign-born children by the thousands each year—a rate that has tripled in the last decade.

But with close to 120,000 children waiting in the U.S. foster care system, what is driving the push in overseas adoptions? It's an emotional issue that goes to the heart of what people are seeking when they adopt a child—and the obstacles they can face in this country.

"I'm happy to see any child adopted anywhere in the world," says Gloria Hochman of the National Adoption Center, based in Philadelphia. "But every time I see a story about a celebrity adopting, I always think, 'Why don't they look here?' It makes me wonder: Do they know there are children waiting here?"

Americans now adopt some 23,000 children overseas every year, according to immigration statistics. Domestically, numbers are difficult to come by. The best estimate is about 13,000–14,000 infant adoptions, and 52,000 child welfare adoptions—the vast majority of those by foster parents or relatives, according to the Evan B. Donaldson Adoption Institute. (The numbers do not include adoptions by stepparents, about 40 percent of all adoptions.)

One key factor in rising international adoptions is that the supply of healthy U.S. infants has been dwindling for decades. Birth control and legal abortions have reduced the number of unwanted births. And our values have changed: The stigma attached to unwed mothers has been greatly reduced, so more mothers are keeping their babies.

Supply has diminished, but demand is strong: Mothers are waiting longer to start families, meaning they may find themselves unable to conceive. And the majority of families considering adoption want infants; it is the closest thing to having one's own baby, to make an imprint from the start of life, to experience each stage of childhood.

The rise in foreign adoptions is just one part of what Adam Pertman, executive director of the Donaldson Institute, calls a "revolution" in adoption. "Many kids do not look like their parents," says Pertman, author of *Adoption Nation: How the Adoption Revolution Is Transforming America*. "New cultures are coming into peoples' homes. People are understanding that families can be formed in different ways." Gay adoptions are another part of this revolution.

As to whether families should focus more on needy children here at home, Pertman says all kids need homes. "Turning it into a competition isn't right for anyone involved," he says.

The top source for Americans is by far China, where there were about 8,000 adoptions (virtually all female) to U.S. families in 2005. Adopting from China "is a more viable option for many people," says Lacee Steigerwald, outreach director for the Great Wall China Adoption agency in Austin, Texas. She says people often come to her agency after frustrating experiences trying to adopt domestically, often when birth parents have changed their minds. "People come to us with horror stories," Steigerwald said. "They've been let down one, two or three times."

In interviews, a number of families echoed that concern about domestic adoption—that they would become emotionally or financially invested, only to have a birth parent change their mind. (All states have different laws defining how long a birth parent has to change their mind, ranging from 0 to 45 days.)

"One of the things parents want is the finality that this is their child," says Will Ahern of Chanhassen, Minnesota. He and his wife adopted their daughter, Summer, now 8, from

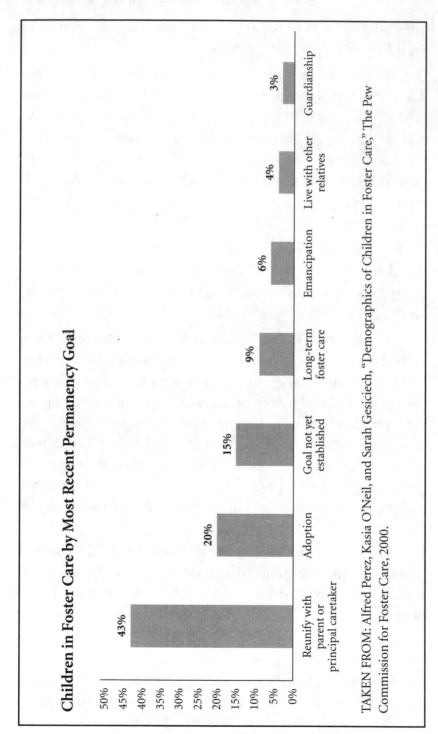

Children in Foster Care by Most Recent Permanency Goal

Category	Percentage
Reunify with parent or principal caretaker	43%
Adoption	20%
Goal not yet established	15%
Long-term foster care	9%
Emancipation	6%
Live with other relatives	4%
Guardianship	3%

TAKEN FROM: Alfred Perez, Kasia O'Neil, and Sarah Gesiciech, "Demographics of Children in Foster Care," The Pew Commission for Foster Care, 2000.

China at 15 months, and he says the process has been "perfect"—"every morning I wake up and celebrate how cool it is."

Kathy Bargar and her husband also chose China when they were ready to adopt. In May, the couple from Danville, California, brought home bright-eyed Gracie, now 2, who had been abandoned at birth in front of an auto parts store in the city of Chengdu—accompanied only by a note, on which was written her birth date and gender.

"We chose China because it's a stable, predictable program," Bargar said. But also, the couple feared domestic adoption might be difficult—partly because they already had one biological daughter, and they thought they might be less marketable to a birth mother, who might think they would favor their biological child. Also, she says, "America views the birth mother as having the first right to a child."

Now, thrilled to have Gracie, Bargar says she would consider all options if she adopts again. "I didn't want the involvement of a birth mother, but now I see how it could be helpful and wonderful," she said.

Some parents throw themselves into the culture of the country they have chosen. Allison von Gruenigen, of Knoxville, Tennessee, is awaiting news from China within days. To prepare, the 45-year-old single-mom-to-be has been attending Chinese New Year celebrations, dance festivals, and language classes. She gets huge support from an ever-growing national network of parents who have adopted in China.

"It was a natural choice to go through China," says von Gruenigen, who has a Chinese-born niece. But she is keeping her mind open for the future. "I know how many kids domestically need a home," she says. "If I see that I'm doing a good job, I might adopt here at some point."

Proponents of domestic adoption acknowledge that huge obstacles exist for families willing to adopt older children. In Georgia, Andrea Shoemaker works for the group Wednesday's

Child, making three-minute films for local TV about kids waiting to be adopted, most ages 8–18.

"We have a lot of families who are willing to step up to the plate," Shoemaker says. "But they get frustrated. The process is difficult. We're not really doing our job to nurture these families, train them, help them before things get too difficult."

Janice Goldwater can attest to that. Goldwater and her husband decided to add to their family when the first of their three natural children went off to college. They adopted Elyana, then almost 10. The child had been removed from her birth family in Siberia for abuse and neglect, then spent three and a half years in an orphanage there. She then was adopted by a New York family that was ill-prepared and could not keep her.

"There have been lots of challenges helping her heal and teaching her to love and to trust," says Goldwater, of Silver Spring, Maryland, who is a founder of the Adoptions Together agency. "It's been very, very hard and very, very valuable."

In the adoption process, Goldwater said she was "shocked at how many roadblocks we came up against." Workers were overloaded with cases. It was hard to find the kids in the system. They considered one child, but relatives in the military expressed interest, so it fell through. Then, the relatives never followed through.

Goldwater supports foreign adoptions, but worries that some high-profile celebrity adoptions might be for the wrong reasons. "People shouldn't adopt to make a political statement," she says.

One of the most moving moments for her, she says, was the moment she was looking for something to write on a card announcing Elyana's adoption. Elyana said maybe she could help, and she composed a poem on the spot.

"First my heart said never," read the closing lines. "But now we are a family forever."

Periodical Bibliography

The following articles have been selected to supplement the diverse views presented in this chapter.

Pal Ahluwalia — "Negotiating Identity: Post-Colonial Ethics and Transnational Adoption," *Journal of Global Ethics*, vol. 3, no. 1, April 2007.

Kevin Minh Allen — "The Price We All Pay: Human Trafficking in International Adoption," *Conducive*, August–September 2009.

E.J. Graff — "Out of Cambodia," *Washington Post*, January 9, 2009.

Jodi Kim — "An 'Orphan' with Two Mothers: Transnational and Transracial Adoption, the Cold War, and Contemporary Asian American Cultural Politics," *American Quarterly*, vol. 61, no. 4, December 2009.

Tara Laskowski — "Examining the Faces of Transnational and Transracial Adoptions," *Mason Gazette*, February 16, 2009.

Susannah Meadows — "The Power of Two," *Newsweek*, December 3, 2009. www.newsweek.com.

Patricia J. Meier — "Small Commodities: How Child Traffickers Exploit Children and Families in Intercountry Adoption and What the United States Must Do to Stop Them," *Journal of Gender, Race, and Justice*, September 22, 2008.

Pamela Anne Quiroz — "Transnational Adoption: Reflections of the 'Diaper Diaspora,'" *International Journal of Sociology and the Social Policy*, vol. 28, no. 11/12, 2008.

Nadirah Sabir — "Finding Families: Should Race Play a Role in Adoption Policies?" *Black Enterprise*, October 2008.

CHAPTER 4

What Changes Should Be Made to the International Adoption Process?

Chapter Preface

One of the puzzling statistics associated with international adoption is the gender preference shown by American adoptive parents toward female babies and children. As statistical information from the Immigration and Naturalization Service (now U.S. Citizenship and Immigration Services) shows, girls make up 64 percent of all children adopted from outside the United States. Many commentators have speculated on the reason for such a lopsided preference for females. No matter the reason, gender preferences in international adoption have had real consequences across the globe.

When prospective adoptive parents register at an agency that specializes in international adoption, they are asked to express a gender preference for the child they hope to adopt. Overwhelmingly, most parents state they would prefer to adopt a female baby or young child. What is it about female children that makes them a more desirable choice?

Some commentators speculate that it has something to do with the available supply of adoptable children. In China, for example, discriminatory and invasive government policies limit each set of parents to one child. As a result of the one-child policy, parents prefer male to female for a number of reasons: Historically, boys were expected to support the family or boys could help out on the family farm or in the family business. Culturally and economically, boys were preferred in China for many years. This meant that female babies were sometimes the victim of infanticide or were abandoned at orphanages. It has been reported that 95 percent of the Chinese children available for adoption were female.

A number of commentators, however, have refuted that reason for American adoptive preferences. Although in China and other Asian countries there is a surplus of girls available for adoption, in other parts of the world the ratio between girls and boys is even—or even favors boys in some countries.

Because these American adoptive gender preferences go back years—reportedly back to the early years of the twentieth century, when records began to be kept on the topic—some commentators perceive the preference to be cultural in nature. Adoptive couples prefer girls because they believe girls will be easier to raise or that the adoptive mother determines the gender of the child—and prefers a girl.

Whatever the reason, gender preferences have real consequences. With kidnapping, baby buying, fraud, and child trafficking a real problem in the international adoption business, the preference for girls can often lead to unsavory acts by unscrupulous adoption agencies to procure female babies for hopeful American couples.

Acknowledging and confronting the issue of gender preferences is one of the issues explored in this chapter, which offers viewpoints that discuss possible changes that can be made to the international adoption process. Other viewpoints examine how the United States should deal with the regulatory issue and with countries that skirt adoptive laws such as the Convention on Protection of Children and Co-operation in Respect of Intercountry Adoption (the Hague Convention on Intercountry Adoption).

> *"Adoptee advocacy groups recommend regulating international laws to help safeguard adoptees, adoptive parents and birth parents in the interest of protecting all groups in the entire adoptive family."*

There Should Be More Regulations in International Adoption

Natalie Cherot

Natalie Cherot is a sociology professor at the University of California, Santa Barbara. In the following viewpoint, she maintains that the 1993 Hague Convention on Protection of Children and Co-operation in Respect of Intercountry Adoption is a much-needed step in the regulation of international adoption. Cherot claims that more regulations—or enforcing rules already in existence—will go a long way in cleaning up the corruption infecting the adoption process in recent years.

As you read, consider the following questions:

1. In 2006, how many of the babies born in Guatemala were adopted into American homes?

2. What does the 1993 Hague Convention on Protection of Children and Co-operation in Respect of Intercountry Adoption do?

3. How long did it take the United States to ratify the Hague Convention after signing it in 1994?

When the topic of enforcing international adoption laws comes up, people usually assume it involves irregularities in the adoption process, including kidnapping and coercing birth parents to give up their babies.

This is what has happened in Guatemala, where an estimated 1 percent of the country's total babies born in 2006 landed in American homes as a result of lenient regulations and a lack of government oversight. In the African country of Chad, six members of a French charity received stiff prison sentences in December for allegedly stealing children who had parents with the intent of passing them off as orphans from Darfur.

But there are other inequities, such as the obstacles faced by many potential adoptive parents, and there are the concerns of adult adoptees, who can offer their own special insight into a process they don't always wish to see continued.

The Hague Convention

In December [2007], the United States ratified a set of regulations that will aid in preventing unethical adoption practices and child trafficking. The U.S. joined 70 other nations in recognizing the 1993 Hague Convention on Protection of Children and Co-operation in Respect of Intercountry Adoption. The convention's 48 articles cover areas such as accrediting the agencies that handle the adoption, maintaining records about the child and the child's birth parents, providing counseling before the adoption and preventing "improper financial gain" from the adoption.

Although adoptee advocates argue that the convention is just a start in protecting children from trafficking, it is in the adoptees', adoptive parents' and birth parents' interest to ensure the U.S. institutes the regulations that the convention requires.

In the weeks leading up to the U.S. ratification, newspapers published human interest stories about couples whose adoptions from Vietnam were being delayed by the U.S. government. One reason is that their adoption files had irregularities, which the U.S. Department of State and the U.S. Embassy were starting to take more seriously than their Vietnamese counterparts.

Potential adoptive parents were uncertain whether the problems would be resolved. They have done the work to prepare to adopt a child internationally. Having paid their fees, traveled around the world to pick up whom they believed to be their new sons or daughters only to see them in limbo and unable to get back to the U.S., tested their resolve. These potential adoptive parents started to demand that the U.S. government make exceptions for these children, insisting that they had done all the required bureaucratic tasks to make these children's adoptions legal.

Adopting a child from Vietnam generally takes almost a year, or more. During this period of rigorous paperwork, weary waiting and figuring out how to pay for five-figure adoption fees, they become much attached to the child they hope to adopt long before that child arrives in their home.

Concerns of Adult Adoptees

Another human face to this story is the adult adoptees, whose lives are often shadowed by adoptive parents' concerns. Many are pushing to enforce international adoption laws, even

---

Best Interests of Child

The overriding need is to ensure that intercountry adoption is only carried out in the best interests of the child. For that to happen, governments of both sending and receiving countries work together to put an end to the corruption that has damaged the image of intercountry adoption and everyone involved—especially the children.

Mac Margolis, "Baby Backlash,"
Newsweek, January 27, 2008. www.newsweek.com.

---

though relaxed standards may have enabled their own adoption. I have been studying the community of Vietnamese adoptees born during the Vietnam War and adopted by American families. The adult adoptees have discussed and written about various adoption concerns, often centered on the lack of racial education they received from white parents or on their desire to return to the nation of their birth. They note the apparent favoritism exhibited in the case of actors Angelina Jolie and Brad Pitt, who received their Vietnamese son after 10 months of paperwork—the barest minimum of delay—when it takes most prospective adoptive parents much longer to complete the process during those precious first year or two of the baby's life.

Adoptee advocacy groups recommend regulating international laws to help safeguard adoptees, adoptive parents and birth parents in the interest of protecting all groups in the entire adoptive family. Potential parents can choose to adopt with countries that have signed and are enforcing the convention.

When reports of corruption surfaced regarding Guatemalan adoptions, the State Department advised U.S. citizens to refrain from adopting from the Central American country until it agrees to comply with the convention (scheduled for early 2008).

Guatemala is not the only country accused of dragging its feet in respect to the Hague Convention. Because of individual state governments, it took 14 years for the U.S. to ratify the convention after originally signing on in 1994.

But, such as other international laws, the convention will be difficult to police. This is especially true in the U.S., where enforcement involves close coordination between individual states.

The Truth About Many Orphanages

As part of a potential adoptive parent's education, he or she should be made aware not all children living in orphanages are legally "orphans," which is commonly understood to be a child with deceased biological parents. An orphanage is sometimes described as a "nursery" because many of the children's parents have not consented to an adoption of their children, and only plan for them to live there temporarily. Orphanages are considered charities where impoverished parents can place children if they cannot afford to feed them or pay for child care while they are working. Because the institutions often provide education, they function more like subsidized boarding schools.

Making sure that the child in the nursery has parents that agreed to the adoption can hold up the adoption for many months.

Many of the adult Vietnamese adoptees whom I interviewed for my research remember their Vietnamese parents visiting them in the nursery before they were sent to the U.S. It was apparent that these parents did not simply discard their children. They made a huge sacrifice to place their child's most critical and immediate needs over their desire to have their children with them.

Several of these adult adoptees eventually found out that their birth parents did not actually consent to their adoption. This knowledge is a terrible burden for them to carry, since they have to take on the difficult task of reconciling this information of their past with their present lives in their adoptive families.

Adoptee advocacy groups have begun letter writing to support the convention and urging adoptive parents to do the same. They argue that it is in the best interest of the adoptee and adoptive parents to avoid potential pain and guilt by supporting the convention's tighter international adoption laws. Most of the adult adoptees I have spoken to are emotionally moved about these children left in limbo and do not wish to see prospective adoptive parents become victims of fraud or extortion.

More Regulations in Everyone's Interests

It should come as no surprise that adult adoptees desire to look at their adoption files, search for biological parents, or question the larger ramifications of international adoption. Some of them want to eliminate international adoption all together. They cite many reasons, one of which is that sending children abroad will not fix the root cause of poverty that created the conditions for their parents to give up their children in the first place.

Adoptee advocacy groups who support international adoption argue that adoptive parents and adult adoptees share the same interest in enforcing convention regulations. They foresee that if adopted children explore their own past it will be devastating for them and their adoptive parents to find out that their birth parents did not consent to their adoption. For these groups, getting the U.S. to sign the convention was the first step.

Adoptee advocacy groups acknowledge that international adoption mostly involves white parents adopting children of color, and they recommend incorporating race-conscious education along with provisions for post-adoption counseling. Adoption agencies should receive proper accreditation and transparency, especially financial transparency. They contend that adoption agencies should be able to make a clear financial trace of the child's life from their birth parents to their adoptive parents without significant gaps and questions arising. Finally, every adoption agency should provide clear information about where adoption fees of up to $30,000 are spent.

For more information about the ethical conduct of adoption, potential adoptive parents can go to Ethica's Web site. Ethica is a research and policy institution—not affiliated with any adoption agency—whose goal is to protect adoptive parents from adoption fraud and trafficking. Ethica's Web site has the most up-to-date information about State Department warnings, Hague Convention violations and adoption industry irregularities.

> "Many [adoptable children] could have found a home in the U.S. if only government—American and Guatemalan—had stayed out of the way."

There Should Be Fewer Regulations in International Adoption

John Stossel

John Stossel is a syndicated columnist and journalist with a show on the FOX Business Network. In the following viewpoint, he asserts that although it is understandable that the U.S. government wants to rid the international adoption process from corruption and adoption fraud, allowing the governments to get involved is not the right answer. Stossel notes that government services are often corrupt and inefficient, and private adoption agencies should be allowed to function without excessive regulation to make a tidy profit.

As you read, consider the following questions:

1. Of more than one hundred cases of alleged baby stealing in Guatemala, how many turned out to be true?

2. What are the top three countries that send children to the United States for adoption?

3. According to Transparency International, Guatemala ranks in what position on the list of corrupt nations in the world?

Do you want to rescue an abandoned child and give him a loving home?

Don't even try, says the U.S. State Department.

That's not exactly what the bureaucrats said, but it's close. The State Department says the Guatemalan adoption system "unduly enriches" so-called baby brokers and that "Guatemala has not established the required central authority to oversee intercountry adoption."

"Central authority"? This from *our* government? They sound like Soviet apparatchiks [officials of the Communist Party].

Last December, the U.S. consul even butted his way into the Guatemalan Congress to make sure a sweeping new adoption law was up to American standards. The law is designed to put those profit-making brokers out of business by making adoption a government monopoly. But to thousands of kids awaiting adoption, a government monopoly could be a death sentence.

Guatemala Is an Adoption Success Story

Yes, there have been horror stories about adoption fraud. Some children were stolen from families. This is horrible, but far from the norm. Out of more than 100 cases of alleged "baby stealing," only five were confirmed as true, says Guatemalan journalist Marta Yolanda Díaz-Durán. That's five crimes versus about 4,000 legal adoptions from Guatemala in 2006 alone. Guatemala has been the second leading source of adopted children coming to America—after China and ahead of Russia. The adoption-broker system—which relied on entrepreneurs providing a service for a fee—worked well enough that Guatemala was an adoption success story.

American adoption agencies (charging a fee) worked with Guatemalan adoption brokers (also charging a fee) to match willing couples with the right children. There was a near-perfect safeguard against baby stealing: two rounds of DNA tests to prove the biological mother gave consent.

The process wasn't cheap—parents paid $25,000 or more, and brokers who spent months or years jumping though the bureaucratic hoops—made, horrors, profit! Hence our State Department's outrage about adoptions that "unduly enrich." The sentiment was captured perfectly by a UNICEF [United Nations Children's Fund] representative who huffed to the *New York Times* that adoption "has become a business instead of a social service."

Government Should Not Be Involved

Oh, yes, everyone loves "social service." But when adoption was a government-run social service in Guatemala, the results were disastrous.

I happened to be in Guatemala City last month [January 2008] visiting the Americas' most free-market university, Universidad Francisco Marroquín [UFM]. UFM's president took me to visit Inés Ayau, a nun who runs an orphanage that was formerly in the hands of the government. The children are well cared for now, but before her church took over, Ayau said, the government staff had forced some children into prostitution. The orphanage itself was rat-infested and without electricity, and the government used the facility to funnel money to cronies. "Thirty-six persons were working, (but) 105 were on the payroll."

Yet U.S. officials want adoption back in the hands of government?!

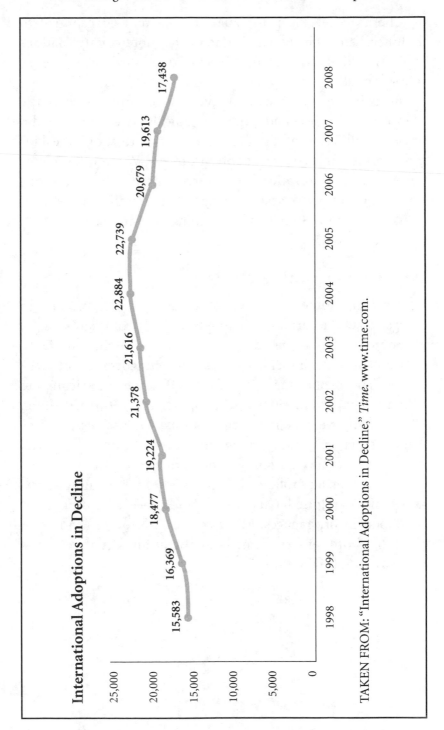

International Adoptions in Decline

15,583
16,369
18,477
19,224
21,378
21,616
22,884
22,739
20,679
19,613
17,438

1998 1999 2000 2001 2002 2003 2004 2005 2006 2007 2008

25,000
20,000
15,000
10,000
5,000
0

TAKEN FROM: "International Adoptions in Decline," *Time.* www.time.com.

There's little reason to expect the current government to do much better. Guatemala is one of the more corrupt nations in the world, 111th out of 179 countries, says Transparency International.

Even if the new bureaucracy isn't corrupt, there's little chance it will process adoptions as quickly as the brokers did because without profit, it has no incentive to move the kids through the cumbersome adoption process. When other countries have put adoption in government hands, adoptions slowed or stopped. Paraguay went from sending more than 400 kids to the U.S. in 1996 to sending zero in 2006.

That's a tragedy.

What's Wrong with Profit?

It may make some people uncomfortable that a middleman charges $5,000 to arrange an adoption, but profit isn't evil.

Someone has to be compensated for arranging the DNA tests and leading hopeful parents past the government's obstacles. The orphanages need funds. If some Americans are willing to pay even $50,000 to adopt, that's not a bad thing. NGOs [nongovernmental organizations], politicians and bureaucrats may call it disgusting "human trafficking," but I call it finding love for children who desperately need it.

Guatemala has followed America's lead, and now thousands of abandoned Guatemalan kids face spending their childhood in orphanages. Many could have found a home in the U.S. if only government—American and Guatemalan— had stayed out of the way.

> "Where the law permits orphanages to become profit centers generating wealth far beyond normal compensation for services, the concept of 'payment for services' is a legal fiction ineffectively hiding a commercial trade in children."

The International Adoption Process Requires More Vigilance Against Child Trafficking

David M. Smolin

David M. Smolin is a professor of law at Cumberland School of Law at Samford University. In the following viewpoint, he posits that a legal argument can be made that international adoptions are a form of child trafficking because the law's distinction between buying children and paying for adoption services is illusory at best.

As you read, consider the following questions:

1. What was Judge Richard Posner's argument in defense of baby selling?

David M. Smolin, "Intercountry Adoption as Child Trafficking," *Valparaiso University Law Review*, vol. 39, Winter 2005, pp. 281, 321–325. Copyright © 2004 Valparaiso University. All rights reserved. Reproduced by permission.

2. What does the author believe can prevent adoption systems from becoming markets in children?

3. According to estimates, what percentage of nations participating in international adoptions have shut down their adoption services because of corruption and child-trafficking scandals?

The fundamental legal distinction between a legitimate adoption and the illicit sale of a child is unclear in both theory and practice. The distinction is maintained by a logically arbitrary system of labeling under which exchanges involving money are classified as legitimate or illegitimate. This labeling system unfortunately appears quite illusory because the distinction between legitimate and illegitimate is maintained by applying conclusory legal labels without a clear relationship to the actual nature of the underlying transaction. Thus, the domestic system of adoption generally labels financial benefits provided to the birth parent, and the birth parent's consent to adoption, as unrelated "gift" and "consent." This labeling is applied even where it is clear that the financial assistance is induced by the representation that the birth parent currently intends to place the child with those providing the "gift." The law deliberately obscures the true nature of the transaction through labels like "gift" to theoretically maintain the rule against selling children. Similarly, the system maintains the illusion that intermediaries are being paid for "services," rather than for the child, even when the payments are contingent on successful delivery of the child or differ according to the characteristics of the child, rather than according to the services rendered.

Posner's Defense

This terminological sleight of hand can be played to the point where child selling can be explicitly defended. The best illustration of this is the famous (or infamous) defense of child selling by Judge Richard Posner, who argued that the law should permit birth parents to sell their infants to adoptive families. Judge Posner defended his proposal by claiming that it did not really amount to "baby selling" since it was merely custodial rights, rather than children, that would be sold. From Judge Posner's perspective, so long as children are not reduced to the status of slaves, they are not being sold. Hence, Judge Posner responded to the criticism that his proposal commodified human beings, or undermined the ban against slavery, by stating that his critics were really confused by the "misuse" of the term "baby selling." Once one used the proper term of "sale of parental rights," all such moral objections should disappear, according to Judge Posner.

One could summarize the word games and arbitrary distinctions of both Judge Posner, and our legal system, as follows:

	Prohibited	Permitted
Judge Posner	Sale of children (as slaves)	Sale of parental or custodial rights
Current law	Sale of children, parental, or custodial rights	"Gifts" to birth parents, Birth parent "expenses," Payment for "services"

My argument is that the law's distinction between illicit sale of children (or parental rights) and licit "gifts," "expenses," and "services" is just as illusory as Judge Posner's distinction between illicit sale of children and licit sale of parental rights. Just as Judge Posner's proposal to permit the sale of parental rights would render a prohibition of baby selling illusory, the law's current permission of "gifts," "expenses," and "services" makes the law's prohibition of selling parental rights and children largely illusory.

The Legal Fiction of "Payment for Services"

I am not arguing that gifts to birth parents, birth parent expenses, or adoption service fees, are in themselves necessarily unethical or tantamount to baby selling. However, the context in which the law permits these activities renders them questionable and allows children to be commercialized and commodified. Thus, in the context of intercountry adoption, it is illusory to distinguish between buying children, and paying for adoption services, when the law has no effective system of preventing adoption intermediaries from profiteering from adoption.

Where the law permits orphanages to become profit centers generating wealth far beyond normal compensation for services, the concept of "payment for services" is a legal fiction ineffectively hiding a commercial trade in children. Where the law permits adoptive parents to be charged for "orphanage donations," but has no effective means of ensuring that these funds are spent on children, rather than being pocketed by intermediaries, "donations" become a legal fiction facilitating a trade in children. Similarly, the distinction between gifts to birth parents and illicitly inducing consent through financial consideration has little meaning in an intercountry adoption system in which aid to assist birth families to stay together is not required and in which it is permissible to offer aid only to birth parents who consent to adoption.

The Illusory Ethics of International Adoption

Thus, where parents give up their children for the lack of a few hundred dollars, or less, but the intercountry adoption system spends tens of thousands of dollars completing the adoption of the child, the concept of compassionate adoption becomes a cruel hoax. Moreover, where impoverished parents in developing nations are offered financial assistance only when they relinquish their children, and the law considers this a licit "gift" unless agency and parent virtually confess to intending a sale, as a result a ban on child selling becomes illusory. Similarly, within the domestic system the concept of pay-

Child Trafficking by Region, 2000	
Region (source)	**Trafficked children**
Asia Pacific	250,000
Latin America + Caribbean	550,000
Africa	200,000
Transition economies	200,000
Developed, industrialized economies	n/a
Total (rounded)	**1,200,000**

TAKEN FROM: International Labour Organization, *Training Manual to Fight Trafficking in Children for Labour, Sexual and Other Forms of Exploitation*, September 2009.

ing for services, but not for children, becomes illusory when agencies charge far more for high-demand white infants, evidencing the development of a market in children. The willingness of the law to label such an obvious sign of a market as a mere "payment of permissible services" indicates that the adoption system is mired in legal fictions with little relationship to the underlying commodification of children.

Thus, adoption can only maintain a principled and enforceable line against child selling and child trafficking when effective systems of enforceable regulation are in place that effectively prevent adoption systems from becoming markets in children. The refusal or failure of the domestic and intercountry adoption systems to put those needed regulations into place speaks volumes regarding the ethics of the domestic and intercountry adoption systems. Unfortunately, upon closer examination it appears that the ethics of the adoption systems, both domestic and intercountry, are just as illusory and fictional as the legal prohibitions on child selling.

International Adoption Is Child Trafficking

If my argument is correct, then those who label intercountry adoption as a form of child trafficking are largely correct, at least under current circumstances and contexts. Intercountry adoption is a form of child trafficking not because adoptive families in rich countries obtain poor children from developing and transition economy nations. Rather, intercountry adoption is a form of child trafficking because the law and current systems of intercountry adoption permit it to operate as such.

I am not arguing that every individual adoption in the current intercountry adoption system constitutes the illicit sale of a child or illicit child trafficking. I am confident that there are many intercountry adoptions that are ethical, where money has not played any improper or illicit role. Moreover, some of the most important sending nations are free of significant child trafficking within their adoption systems. However, the system as a whole is corrupt because it has no effective means of preventing intercountry adoption from degenerating into illicit child trafficking. This legal failure, moreover, is not merely a theoretical difficulty. According to one estimate, over forty percent of significant sending nations over the last fifteen years have been shut down due primarily to adoption scandals concerning corruption and child trafficking. This estimate, moreover, does not include nations, such as India, that have been plagued by significant adoption scandals but have not experienced a nationwide shutdown or moratorium. The gaps in the law, therefore, are accompanied by recurrent and systematic baby-selling scandals. Moreover, these abusive adoption practices are not new but have been going on for decades. The problems with intercountry adoption and child trafficking are systematic and recurrent, not exceptional or occasional.

Reforms in the System Are Needed

Of course, it could be argued that the very nature of intercountry adoption, involving a transaction between rich and poor nations, lends itself to abuse, and therefore the choice is ultimately between shutting down intercountry adoption, or allowing it to continue, in the interests of saving children, despite these abuses. This kind of argument implicitly justifies child trafficking in the name of the best interest of the child. Such justifications are not of the explicit sort provided by Judge Posner but rather of the apologetic, "we just can't stop it," variety. From this perspective, child selling in the guise of adoption becomes a kind of vice crime, like gambling or prostitution, that the law is helpless to stop and that may cause more harm than good to prevent. It is against this kind of argument that . . . [this viewpoint is] directed. Child trafficking is not a mere "vice" crime that the law may legalize, regulate, or allow to operate in the shadows. Child trafficking is a profound violation of human rights that law and society must energetically seek to abolish, wherever it may be found and whatever disguises it may adopt. Further, as this [viewpoint] makes clear, the law has in no way exhausted the regulatory possibilities for preventing intercountry adoption from degenerating into a form of trafficking. Only when the law has energetically implemented the obvious and rational regulatory steps to prevent adoption as trafficking can the argument be made that the only choices are banning intercountry adoption or permitting trafficking. Indeed, it is those supposed advocates of intercountry adoptions who resist such regulations and excuse the presence of trafficking in the adoption system, who are digging the grave of intercountry adoption.

Intercountry adoption is a conditional good; intercountry adoption as child trafficking is an evil. Only when the law, society, and intercountry adoption system are reformed will the conditions under which intercountry adoption can flourish as a good be established. Unfortunately, the prospects for such reform are poor because there are few within the current intercountry adoption system with the motivation to demand it. Hence, the recurrent cycle of scandal, excuse, and ineffective "reform" will probably continue until intercountry adoption is finally abolished, with history labeling the entire enterprise as a neocolonialist mistake. It does not have to be this way, but it will take more than legal fictions and illusory restrictions on child trafficking to prevent the ultimate demise of the inter-country adoption system.

> *"By prohibiting U.S. agencies from partaking in adoptions with entities that have engaged in exploitative practices, the United States can motivate agencies in foreign countries to choose safe adoption processes."*

The United States Should Not Deal with Countries That Exploit Children and the International Adoption Process

Kate O'Keefe

Kate O'Keefe is an attorney. In the following viewpoint, she asserts that the United States should refrain from dealing with countries that abuse the international adoption process and encourage countries that haven't ratified the Hague Convention on Protection of Children and Co-operation in Respect of Intercountry Adoption to follow its rules by offering incentives to do so. O'Keefe believes that the United States can motivate countries to implement safe adoption practices.

Kate O'Keefe, "The Intercountry Adoption Act of 2000: The United States' Ratification of the Hague Convention on the Protection of Children, and Its Meager Effect on International Adoption," *Vanderbilt Journal of Transnational Law*, November 1, 2007. Copyright © 2007 Vanderbilt University Law School. Reproduced by permission.

As you read, consider the following questions:

1. In 2006, how many children were adopted into the United States from the top twenty sending countries?

2. How many of these adoptions would have been covered under the Hague Convention?

3. In 2006, how many children were adopted from Russia and South Korea, neither of which have signed on to the Hague Convention?

It stands to be seen what effect the United States' ratification [in 2007] of the Hague Convention [on Protection of Children and Co-operation in Respect of Intercountry Adoption], through the implementation of the IAA [the Intercountry Adoption Act of 2000] will have on the safety of the intercountry adoption process for the children involved. Two inherent issues in the fundamentals of the Hague Convention may hinder the usefulness of the legislation as it now stands: (1) the standards of the Hague Convention do not apply where only one of the countries involved in an adoption is a party to the Convention; and (2) the required establishment of a central authority to oversee the regulation of adoptions may prove to be an insurmountable hurdle in some countries where the adoption process is most in need of repair.

The Hague Convention states explicitly that it applies only when an adoption involves a child from a country that is a party to the Convention who is being adopted by someone in another country that is a party to the Convention. The Hague Convention does not prohibit contracting parties from participating in adoptions with nonparty countries where the requirements of the Convention do not apply. The IAA contains no limit on adoptions with nonparty countries either, its purposes being limited to implementing the Hague Convention in the United States and protecting the rights of the parties involved in adoptions "subject to the Convention."

This provision greatly weakens the effect of the IAA, as the United States currently participates in adoptions with many countries that are not parties to the Convention. Of the 19,797 children that were adopted into the United States in 2006 from the top twenty sending countries, only 7,848 of their adoptions would have been covered by the Hague Convention had the IAA already been in effect in the United States.

United States Does Business with Countries That Violate Treaty

Since 1997, the top four countries from which families in the United States have adopted have been China, Russia, South Korea, and Guatemala. Of these four, only China has ratified the Hague Convention and is in good standing; Guatemala is a party to the Convention, but is currently in violation of its standards; Russia signed the Convention in 2000 but has not yet ratified it; and South Korea has neither signed nor ratified the Convention.

New Jersey Representative Christopher Smith, who in November of 2006 chaired the discussion of the Hague Convention in the hearing of the Africa, Global Human Rights, and International Operations Subcommittee of the House Committee on [Foreign Affairs], addressed the "serious concerns about things like baby selling and trafficking, abandonment and fraud" that the United States has with regard to the top four sending countries. However, the ratification of the Hague Convention will not alleviate these concerns in connection with South Korea or Russia. Guatemala is currently in violation of the Hague Convention and, thus, once the United States ratifies the Convention, U.S. adoption from that country will be forced to cease until standards are met.

Furthermore, taking evidence from history, a number of countries that are candidates to have an outpouring of adoptable children in the near future due to social, political, and economic upheaval, are also not parties to the Hague Convention. As discussed earlier, many of the countries affected by the tsunami in 2004 closed off their borders to adoption in the wake of the disaster, due in part to the inability to identify whether children were in fact orphans and in part due to fears of trafficking. If those moratoria are lifted, the Hague Convention will only apply in limited circumstances. Indonesia, the country most severely devastated by the tsunami, is not a party to the Convention. Of the eleven countries that suffered fatalities from the tsunami, only Sri Lanka, India, and Thailand are contracting members of the Convention.

As evidenced by past trends, war-ravaged countries often become prime sending countries for intercountry adoptions in the aftermath of conflict. From this standpoint, it can be imagined that countries such as Iraq, Afghanistan, Lebanon, and Israel may have a need for the institution of adoption in the coming years. Of these four countries, only Israel is a contracting member state to the Convention; none of the other three have even indicated an intent to ratify by signing.

The Problem of Sub-Saharan Africa

Perhaps the largest and fastest growing concentration of orphans is in sub-Saharan Africa, where civil war, poverty, and disease are taking an enormous toll on the population. Sub-Saharan Africa is home to over forty-eight million orphans, one-fourth of them orphaned by the AIDS virus. While the total number of orphans in Latin America and Asia has decreased since 1990, the number in sub-Saharan Africa has increased by more than 50% in that same period. An estimated 12% of all children in the area have lost at least one parent, and in eight countries, this number reaches more than 15%. More than half of these children are under the age of twelve, and while many children who lose one parent continue to live with the surviving parent, this is not always the case. Recent data from seven sub-Saharan countries indicate that between 56% and 65% of children who lose their fathers continue to live with their mothers, and only between 25% and 52% of children who lose their mothers continue to live with their fathers.

Between the years 2000 and 2005, more than 40% of deaths occurring in southern Africa were of people between the ages of twenty and thirty-nine, up from just over 10% between 1985 and 1990. Estimates based on current HIV infection rates and the availability of medications indicate that by 2010, sub-Saharan Africa will be home to 53 million orphans, 15.7 million of whom will be orphaned by AIDS.

Traditionally, there was "no such thing as an orphan in Africa," as children were routinely cared for by extended family after losing their parents. While the majority of children who have either lost both parents or are not living with their surviving parent are cared for by other family members, this solution is not as definite as it once was. The increase in the number of orphans and the decrease in the number of available caregivers due to drought, war, and disease are breaking down the once infallible support system of extended family members. Providing for orphans is a strain on families, and studies have shown that orphans are often less likely to possess basic material goods such as shoes, blankets, and extra clothes than other children. Orphans are more likely than their peers to be deprived of education, socialization, and nutrition, and they are more prone to crime, abuse, neglect, child labor, prostitution, HIV infection, depression, and long-term mental health problems. Furthermore, there is some indication that orphaned children experience discrimination in their new homes and are given different food and clothing than other children, especially where resources are particularly scarce.

In some extreme cases, children who do not have extended family able or willing to care for them end up supporting themselves and siblings. Orphans in child-headed households are even more prone to the symptoms listed above than other orphans, often forced to leave school in order to care for younger siblings or earn any small amount of money that will allow for their survival. Africa's urban areas have seen an explosion of homeless youth living on the streets, beginning when coffee prices crashed in the 1980s and many children of large families were forced to go out and make money, and the number of homeless youth grew rapidly due to AIDS and regional conflicts. There is no dependable estimate for how many homeless children there are, but there could be as many as one million living on the city streets, panhandling or shining shoes for money, "vulnerable to drug addiction, bullying, sexual abuse and devastating health conditions." Still other children are forced to live in delinquency homes, temporary makeshift facilities, or institutional settings until a better solution can be found. In some countries, orphanages are overcrowded and unable to accommodate the many children on their waiting lists.

Challenges in African Countries

Limited public funds and the numerous challenges facing the countries of sub-Saharan Africa have contributed to a lack of response to the orphan crisis. Local community-based organizations and nongovernmental organizations have been providing support to children for several years through self-help groups, burial associations, grain-loan schemes, payment of school fees, and supplying food and clothing. While many of these organizations have grown significantly since their inception, inadequate funding keeps them from meeting the need in their communities. Some orphan care programs have been developed at the national level, but financial constraints, lack of awareness about orphans, and the stigma attached to the AIDS virus have limited this trend such that only six countries in sub-Saharan Africa—15% of all countries in the region— had developed programs as of 2003. International support for orphans is a newer development, but many of the agencies involved have little experience in providing support for children, and few of the resources actually reach the neediest communities.

Thus far, most of the funding for orphans in Africa has been directed at easing the strain on families who are supporting their own kin, as has been the tradition in sub-Saharan African countries. However, with the growing numbers of orphans, family members are finding themselves caring for multiple orphans with resources that are seriously inadequate. The traditional family-based system for orphan care is deteriorating, with some extended family members abandoning orphans or fighting over who will bear the burden of them.

Only recently has discussion arisen regarding adoption as an option for African children, as it has never been widely practiced due to the strong network of family care. However, increased need has changed cultural preferences against adoption in other countries and is likely to do the same in sub-Saharan Africa, where the resources in the area simply cannot support the multitude of orphans. The cultural barriers that have prevented non-kin adoptions in the past and the economic strains that are preventing families from supporting their own orphans will likely make any large growth in domestic adoptions difficult to achieve.

Adoption May Open Up in Future

Significant concerns exist regarding the adoption of African children into U.S. homes, stemming largely from the lingering effects of slavery and the importance of maintaining cultural identity. Additionally, certain Islamic countries in Africa may have ethnic and religious restrictions against adoption. However, history indicates that it is fathomable, if not likely, that those in the United States will respond to the current orphan crisis with a willingness to adopt, and that at least some of the cultural aversions to adoption may change. The United States has already seen an increase in adoptions from one African

Convention Countries

Albania	El Salvador	Mongolia
Andorra	Estonia	Netherlands
Armenia	Finland	New Zealand
Australia	France	Norway
Austria	Georgia	Panama
Azerbaijan	Germany	Paraguay
Belarus	Guatemala	Peru
Belgium	Guinea	Philippines
Belize	Hungary	Poland
Bolivia	Iceland	Portugal
Brazil	India	Romania
Bulgaria	Israel	San Marino
Burkina Faso	Italy	Seychelles
Burundi	Kenya	Slovakia
Cambodia	Latvia	Slovenia
Canada	Liechtenstein	South Africa
Chile	Lithuania	Spain
China (and Hong Kong)	Luxembourg	Sri Lanka
Colombia	Macedonia	Sweden
Costa Rica	Madagascar	Switzerland
Cuba	Mali	Thailand
Cyprus	Malta	Turkey
Czech Republic	Mauritius	United Kingdom
Denmark	Mexico	Uruguay
Dominican Republic	Moldova	Venezuela
Ecuador	Monaco	

TAKEN FROM: Office of Children's Issues, U.S. Department of State, 2009.

country, Ethiopia, which sent the fifth-most children to the United States for adoption in 2006. Ethiopia is not, however, a party to the Hague Convention. In fact, of the forty-four countries that make up the area considered sub-Saharan Africa, only eight are parties to the Convention, and not one of the eight countries where the orphan population is at or above fifteen percent has even signed the Convention.

The United States is on the brink of implementing the Hague Convention thirteen years after first indicating its intention to do so, and it is likely to have only a limited effect on intercountry adoptions into the United States. Many of the countries from which Americans adopt, or are likely to do so in the future, are not parties to the Hague Convention. Moreover, the requirements of the Convention will make it difficult to ratify, and with no prohibition on adoptions between contracting and non-contracting countries, there is little incentive for countries to do so. The United States, despite its wealth of resources, took nearly thirteen years to complete the entire process. Many of the countries that are at the forefront of intercountry adoption, or may be in the near future, will likely find the requirements of the Hague Convention impossible to comply with. With governments that are unstable or grappling with war, poverty, unrest, and disease, implementing a central authority, formulating and enforcing an accreditation scheme, and fulfilling the research and reporting requirements before a child can be adopted will be too much of a drain on scarce government resources. The circumstances that make it difficult for these countries to support their children also make the burden of complying with the Convention overwhelming. Without implementation of the Convention, there is no authority ensuring the valid adoptability of children, no restrictions on exorbitant fees for intercountry adoptions, and nothing to prevent the same tragic practices that have been rampant in intercountry adoption in the past.

Solution

Had the IAA been in effect in 2006, it would have governed adoptions from one of the top five sending countries, three of the top ten sending countries, and nine of the top twenty sending countries. Furthermore, judging from historical trends whereby political, social, and economic upheaval has led to an influx of orphans into the United States from afflicted countries, there is distinct potential for an increase in adoptions from countries throughout sub-Saharan Africa and the Middle East that are not parties to the Hague Convention. These countries will likely be unable to become parties to the Convention given its strict bureaucratic and organizational requirements. The result is legislation that will allow thousands of children to be adopted into the United States each year without its protection, potentially taken or purchased from their families unlawfully, and mistreated before being "sold" into adoption. As the country that adopts more children from outside its borders than all other countries in the world combined, the United States has an obligation to protect the children and families involved in adoptions not covered by the Hague Convention, even once the IAA is fully implemented.

One potential solution would be to alter the IAA to prohibit the United States from engaging in adoptions from countries that are not parties to the Convention. Such a tactic has been used by some countries in the past; certain frequent-sending countries who are parties to the Convention have prevented U.S. citizens from adopting their children due to the United States' failure to ratify. Critics of the Hague Convention have pointed to its omission of a similar provision as a major failure in its drafting and an impediment to its successful implementation. Their theory is that such a requirement would "provide an incentive and motivation for both sending and receiving countries to comply with the Hague Convention regulations." According to such a rationale, a prohibition in the IAA would likely have a similar effect to one in the Hague Convention. As the principal receiving country for intercountry adoptions in the world, a threat to the availability of adoptions into the United States would have considerable influence on incentive and motivation for sending countries to ratify the Hague Convention.

Advocating the addition of a prohibition clause into the IAA, however, ignores the difficulty that many countries face in implementing the Hague Convention. In many cases, a failure to ratify is due to inability, not unwillingness. For governments struggling to overcome war, poverty, and disease, complying with the Hague Convention is impossible. A provision in the IAA prohibiting adoptions with countries that are not parties to the Convention would not provide an incentive for ratification, but would effectively shut down the intercountry adoption process, at least into the United States, for countries that may have extreme need.

United States Should Encourage Compliance

Rather than eliminating the possibility of adoption for many countries, the goal of the United States should be to encourage and facilitate adoptions from foreign countries, even those that are not parties to the Hague Convention, when the process is in the best interest of the child. The fact that key sending countries are not parties to the Convention, most notably Russia and South Korea (who sent a combined 5,082 children to the United States in 2006), accentuates the need for the United States to take further measures than those provided for in the IAA. Where sending countries are unable to institute the infrastructure necessary to implement the Hague Convention, the United States must take on more responsibility to ensure the safety and validity of adoptions with such countries.

One solution is to have the State Department and the accredited agencies involved in adoptions with countries that are not parties to the Hague Convention assume the duties that would be performed by the central authority in the sending country if it were a party. In order to participate in adoptions with the United States, sending countries would be required to give representatives from the United States access to the necessary information regarding the adoptability of children. Such a system, however, would prove to be logistically difficult, time consuming, and expensive to maintain. U.S. agencies would have to obtain proof of the adoptability of a child, lack of a domestic option for the child, and all necessary consent. Obtaining this information and ensuring its accuracy would be more difficult for far-removed U.S. authorities than for local ones, especially where the information is not held by the local government, but by agencies and individuals who stand to gain from the child's adoption. It may be complicated for U.S. authorities, who are not familiar with the laws of foreign countries and the forms of documentation issued at birth, to avoid being duped by dishonest parties. Furthermore, the process may be objected to as being an intrusion by U.S. authorities into the privacy of foreign citizens and the dealings of the foreign government or private agencies.

A better tactic is to provide an incentive for individuals involved in the adoption process to comply with the ideals of the Hague Convention rather than an incentive for ratification by the entire country. Where the governments of sending countries are unable to implement the public authority needed to regulate the process and comply with the Hague Convention, the United States must go directly to the source of the exploitation and trafficking problems: the individuals and agencies that profit at the expense of innocent families. Rather than cutting off all adoptions from a country that is not a party to the Convention, the United States should include in the IAA a provision whereby agencies in the United States will be prohibited from engaging in adoption procedures with any foreign entity or individual that has been found to be in violation of the ideals of the Convention. For example, any orphanage, adoption agency, or individual adoption agent in a sending country that is found to be recruiting and purchasing children from their families, taking children under false pretenses, falsifying documents, or receiving "improper financial or other gain" from the sale of children should be permanently prohibited from participating in adoptions with any agency in the United States.

Incentives Work

Critical to the success of such a provision is that the benefits of complying substantially outweigh the potential gains from a violation. The IAA should call for a permanent ban on all future adoptions in return for a single violation, making the repercussions for violation severe enough that being caught would end any and all profits from the large U.S. market. Equally as important is a liberal interpretation of the Convention language allowing for "professional fees for persons involved in the adoption." If agencies stand to make nominal or no profit from intercountry adoptions, the risk of being found in violation of the provision may be worth the potential 1000% markup that some adoptions yield. Some profit must be gained from intercountry adoptions by the entities in the sending country, such that agencies will find it preferable to obey the provisions of the IAA and be assured steady income rather than violate and earn a much larger, but riskier, profit.

To give teeth to such a provision, the State Department must form a relationship with local governments whereby random and periodic investigations of entities can be conducted in nonmember countries. Such investigations should be similar to those conducted in Cambodia in 2002, when the State Department and the immigration services worked with the Cambodian government to uncover the corrupt adoption practices in that country. Cooperation will validate U.S. intrusion upon private entities, and the knowledge and insight of the local governments will make the process run more smoothly. Obviously, there is no realistic way to investigate all entities in all countries with which the United States may interact, and there would be no assurance of compliance. However, a provision whereby agencies in the United States would be prohibited from engaging in adoption procedures with any foreign entity that has been found to be in violation of the ideals of the Convention would act as an incentive to at least some entities to provide adoption services in a manner that protects the safety of the children involved and satisfies the goals of the Hague Convention.

Progress Can Be Made

In the sixty-plus years since its emergence at the end of World War II, intercountry adoption has become a highly popular practice in the United States and one that, when correctly managed, is beneficial to both the children and the adopting families involved. Through intercountry adoption, countless children have been given homes and opportunities that would not have been available to them in their countries of origin.

With the increased popularity of intercountry adoption, however, have come tragic consequences for many children in foreign countries, who are exploited by those involved in the adoption process. While the United States' implementation of the Hague Convention through the IAA is commendable, its effects on the safety of the thousands of foreign-born children who are adopted by U.S. families each year may prove to be very limited. A substantial number of the countries that families in the United States adopt from are not parties to the Convention and, therefore, its protections will not apply to them. Because these countries will likely find it very difficult, if not impossible, to ratify the Convention, and because the availability of adoption is so vital to the children of these countries, the United States must be willing to use its resources to ensure the safety of these adoptions. By prohibiting U.S. agencies from partaking in adoptions with entities that have engaged in exploitative practices, the United States can motivate agencies in foreign countries to choose safe adoption processes, even without the oversight of a central government authority under the Hague Convention.

> "Child care professionals say that, while domestic violence and corruption may be painful realities in cases, Russia's orphans are being used as a political football by nationalist politicians."

International Adoptions Should Not Be Used as a Political Issue

Fred Weir

Fred Weir is a correspondent working for the Christian Science Monitor. *In the following viewpoint, he maintains that recent charges against the Russian adoption process are politically motivated and based on misinformation in some cases. As a result, Weir notes, Russia has severely restricted foreign and domestic adoptions, leaving many eligible children trapped in institutions and prospective American parents empty-handed.*

As you read, consider the following questions:

1. According to estimates, how many children in Russia are orphans?

Fred Weir, "Adoptions from Russia Face a Chill," *Christian Science Monitor*, June 23, 2005, p. 1. Copyright © 2005 The Christian Science Publishing Society. All rights reserved. Reproduced by permission from Christian Science Monitor, (www.csmonitor.com).

2. How many Russian children have been adopted by foreigners from 1995 to 2005?

3. How much do foreigners typically pay in agency fees during the adoption process in Russia?

K errie and Scott Farkas are looking forward to spending their lives with Dmitri, a blond, brown-eyed 2-year-old they've just spent two days with at an orphanage in Tambov, in central Russia.

They're optimistic despite a significant slowdown in international adoptions from Russia this year [2005], due to an ugly and very public bureaucratic war that pits government liberals and child care agencies against nationalist politicians who allege that children are being "trafficked" abroad. If the politicians' demands for change are met, they could severely curtail the ability of prospective foreign parents to adopt here.

Mr. Farkas says that for him and his wife, things are going well so far. "We have a good agency, and they have brought us through any potential problems," he says.

Charges Fly from Russian Officials

Foreign adoption has long been a sensitive issue in Russia, where the population has been shrinking for decades while the number of children without families has ballooned to an estimated 700,000. Last spring, the Russian media heavily covered the case of Irma Pavlis, a Chicago woman sentenced to 12 years in the abuse-related death of her adopted Russian son, Alex, in 2003. The daily *Komsomolskaya Pravda* reported that at least 13 Russian children have been "murdered" by US parents since foreign adoptions became possible in 1990.

In separate incidents this month [June 2005], Moscow police seized adoptive children from two couples, one Italian and one American, after accusations of child abuse were phoned in. Both the US and Italian embassies issued strong statements casting doubt on the charges and warning of political manipulation.

"We heard about these incidents, and we find it inexplicable," says Scott Farkas, who will return to Lancaster, Pa., for a six- to eight-week wait to finalize his own adoption of Dmitri. "We can't understand how someone would go through this process and have that as the result."

Internal Adoptions on the Decline

Some 60,000 Russian children have been adopted by foreigners over the past decade [1995–2005]. Well over half of them have found homes with Americans, who adopted about 23,000 children around the world last year. The Russian figures have spiked in recent years, with nearly 10,000 international adoptions last year, 5,865 of them to the US. The number adopted so far this year has dropped by a third.

Experts say the kind of problems cropping up for prospective parents in Russia have been encountered elsewhere. Adoptions from Vietnam (about 700 annually) halted in 2002 amid charges of corruption and "infant trafficking." A bilateral agreement on adoption concluded between the US and visiting Vietnamese Prime Minister Phan Van Khai on Tuesday may put the process back on track.

A child protection law enacted by Romania in 2002 imposed such onerous restrictions that the practice stopped, leaving thousands of eligible children trapped in institutions. Last week, Ukraine placed a temporary freeze on all international adoptions, pending a government restructuring.

"It's very common in international adoptions that there are starts and stops," says Stephanie Mitchell, executive director of MAPS [Worldwide], an international adoption agency based in Maine. "There's a lot of curiosity in some cultures about why foreigners want to adopt their children, and this can lead to rumors and misconceptions taking hold."

Internal Russian Politics Have Consequences

To some Russians, the spate of child abuse allegations against foreigners appears a timely validation of claims by a group of State Duma deputies that Russia's adoption process, overseen by the Ministry of Education, is riddled with corruption and incompetence, leading to the virtual sale of Russian children.

Yekaterina Lakhova, chair of the Duma's powerful commission on women, family, and youth, told a radio program this week that Russia's adoption system was geared to "selling" children to foreigners rather than finding suitable parents at home for them. Without citing examples, Communist lawmaker Svetlana Goryacheva told parliament last week that Russian children were being "trafficked" to Western pornographers and prostitution rings.

A tough review initiated by Russia's top prosecutor has led to denial of accreditation to at least a dozen of the approximately 80 international adoption agencies working in Russia, and more could face the ax.

"We see many cases of cruel treatment of children by foreign adopters," says Nina Ostanina, deputy chairwoman of Ms. Lakhova's commission. "The Ministry of Education is a corrupted structure. We need them to stop the practice of demanding and receiving money for selling our children abroad. We want to tighten up procedures and conclude bilateral agreements to enable the state to take under control [Russian] adopted children living abroad."

Children as Political Footballs

Child care professionals say that, while domestic violence and corruption may be painful realities in cases, Russia's orphans are being used as a political football by nationalist politicians.

"About 2,000 Russian children perish each year in domestic violence, yet this attracts no media outrage," says Boris Altshuler, head of Child's Rights, a Russian NGO [nongovernmental organization] that works with children. "This is a top-level political game, to which children are hostages. Some powerful forces in Russia want to undermine [President Vladimir] Putin's policies of closer cooperation with the West."

Mr. Altshuler says the harsh review of agencies was uncalled for because most of the high-profile instances of abuse—including the Pavlis case—occurred to children adopted through a loophole in Russian law that permits "independent" adoptions.

"In some regions the process is dominated by middlemen who advertise on the Internet and charge high fees," he says. "They don't face the same legal and documentary requirements as international agencies do, and this has been the source of most of the problems. Our nationalist politicians talk about the need to control Russian children living abroad, but say little about the need to control this mafia at home."

Foreigners who adopt through accredited agencies typically pay about $20,000 in agency fees, travel expenses, and legal and translation costs. According to one expert, agencies usually make a donation to the originating orphanage, but never in cash. The financial outlays made by foreigners are one of the key controversies, since adoption is supposed to be free under Russian law.

Tightening Up the Adoption Process

Following the Pavlis case, nationalist Duma deputies succeeded in cracking down on foreign-based adoption agencies and revising the family code to make international adoptions harder.

Ms. Ostanina says the main reform demanded now by the Duma group, which includes dozens of leading lawmakers, is the conclusion of "bilateral treaties" that will empower Russian officials to follow and intervene in the lives of children who've been adopted by foreigners.

"If these deputies get their way, I'm afraid international adoptions will just come to an end," says Natasha Shaginian-Needham, executive director of New York-based Happy Families International [Center], which was reaccredited after the recent review. "A child adopted by an American family will become a US citizen. There are privacy issues. This seems to be just a way to chill the process."

Child care experts here say domestic adoptions have halved over the past decade, with just 6,000 Russian orphans taken in by Russians last year. "There is a lack of public information, which feeds widely believed stereotypes about orphans being genetically flawed, or destined to become hooligans," says Eric Batsie, Russia director of Kidsave International, an advocacy group that runs a partly US-funded project to promote domestic adoptions.

Domestic Adoption in Russia Suffers

Russians say the process is no easier for them than it is for foreigners. Svetlana Sorokina, a TV news anchor who adopted a girl two years ago, says she searched for more than a year and endured a maze of obstacles. "Even with all my contacts as a journalist I found it very difficult," she says. "Our state does nothing to help."

The Education Ministry, the main target of criticism, is fighting back. This week it launched a Russian-language Web site (www.usinovite.ru) that will provide access to a database of 260,000 Russian orphans, along with information about adoption and a list of accredited agencies. Officials say an English-language version may be added. In an accompanying statement the minister, Andrei Fursenko, warned that "all too often, unfortunate orphans are being used as a pretext for unscrupulous political campaigns. Suffering children shouldn't be the subjects of such speculation."

But many professionals say the atmosphere is unlikely to improve soon. "International adoption has become such a hot potato here that anything that comes up, like the Pavlis case, will lead to more trouble," says Ms. Shaginian-Needham, whose agency sponsors projects to promote domestic as well as foreign adoptions. "Many of us in this field are Russians ourselves, and we wish Russian children could stay at home as much as anyone else does. But there is no alternative to foreign adoptions for now, and if they end, it'll be the children who suffer."

"Due to the small numbers of internationally adopted children in a given medical practice . . . , most providers have not had extensive exposure to . . . the variety of health issues that may affect these children."

There Should Be Pre- and Post-Pediatric Counseling in the International Adoption Process

Sandra L. Iverson and Dana E. Johnson

Sandra L. Iverson is the associate director and Dana E. Johnson is the director of the International Adoption Clinic at the University of Minnesota. In the following viewpoint, they underscore the importance of pre- and post-adoption evaluations for children adopted from overseas. Iverson and Johnson provide an overview of the conditions and factors vital to a thorough evaluative process.

Sandra L. Iverson and Dana E. Johnson, *2005 Report on Intercountry Adoption*. Glastonbury, CT: Adoption Resource of Connecticut, 2005. Copyright © 2005 Adoption Resource Center of Connecticut. Reproduced by permission.

As you read, consider the following questions:

1. Twenty years ago the majority of adopted children came to the United States from what countries?

2. From what countries do the majority of adopted children come today?

3. Why are laboratory screening tests crucial to the initial medical evaluation?

There has been tremendous growth in the number of U.S. families adopting internationally in the past twenty years. Due to the high rate of involuntary infertility along with a decrease in the number of U.S.-born infants available for adoption, international adoptions have increased significantly. While there were about 8,000 children adopted by American families in 1984, that number rose to more than 20,000 in 2002. In addition, the countries from which children are being adopted have also changed during that time. Twenty years ago the majority of children were adopted from Korea with fewer from India, Latin America and the Philippines while at this time most children come from Eastern Europe and China. Children from Korea are usually well cared for in foster homes while most children from Eastern Europe and China have lived in institutions. In institutional care, there often is a lack of medical and financial resources as well as a shortage of caregivers so necessary for normal growth and development of children. Due to the increase in the numbers of international adoptions, most physicians and other primary care providers for children will be caring for these children in their practices. However, due to the small numbers of internationally adopted children in a given medical practice along with the special needs of post-institutionalized children, most providers have not had extensive exposure to the process of international adoption and the variety of health issues that may affect these children.

The Pre-Adoption Evaluation

The purpose of the pre-adoption evaluation is to assist families in choosing a child who they feel capable of parenting. Helping the family understand the specific needs of a given child and assess if they have the desire and resources available to parent that child is crucial in the pre-adoption process. Unfortunately, it is difficult to do a thorough evaluation from afar for a number of reasons.

Usually a family is given a referral packet that contains some information on the background of the child, his present condition and one or two photos or perhaps a video. The medical information that the parents receive varies in quantity and quality. Some international agencies provide extensive information on the biological parents, circumstances surrounding the birth, a medical history of the child, sequential growth parameters and the results of a recent physical examination and developmental assessment. Other times the information may be minimal with only a statement about the child's general health such as "healthy" or "mild developmental delays". The accuracy of the information varies greatly. Children adopted from countries with good medical facilities and well-trained health providers will be able to provide a more thorough health assessment. However, most children arrive from countries and institutions where good medical and diagnostic services may not be available.

Differences in Diagnoses

The referral diagnoses for Eastern European children are very different than are used in Western countries. Common diagnoses include many neurologic terms including "Perinatal Encephalopathy", Hydocephalic Syndrome and Developmental Delays; however, a study found in JAMA [*Journal of the American Medical Association*] by Albers et al. found that although 91% of reviewed referrals from Eastern Europe had neurologic diagnoses on arrival, no child when examined had a neurologic problem although most were developmentally delayed and many had significant undocumented problems.

Countries vary in the amount and type of information that they give to parents before a family commits to a specific child. While a video of a child may be helpful in assessing certain conditions, it is illegal to send videos abroad in some countries. Sometimes a family is given no information until they actually visit the country and choose a child at that time. In this case a family is placed in the difficult and very emotional situation of having to make a lifelong decision far away from home without medical guidance.

Developmental status is difficult to assess from afar. We expect children who have been cared for in institutions to have some delay in all areas of development, large motor, fine motor, speech and emotional. As a general guideline we expect children to have about a one-month delay for each three months in institutional care up to the age of 12 months and then catch up through 18 months. A one-month delay in speech development is common for each three months in institutional care throughout the duration of confinement. Sometimes a videotape of the child may be available. However, a segment of videotape of a child only shows a tiny fraction of the child's life. Generally the video is made to compel rather than inform. It is rarely well enough made or of sufficient quality to assess development. A child's emotional and behavioral as well as cognitive development is almost impossible to assess beforehand. Development will also be affected by child care traditions. Children who are held the majority of time during their first few months of life rather than having the opportunity to explore on their own may develop their milestones in gross motor development somewhat later. This is apparent in children cared for in foster homes in Korea and Guatemala. Once the child is given the opportunity to move around and explore he quickly catches up.

Other Factors in Evaluative Process

Growth information can be very helpful in assessing a child's health. Birth measurements including height, weight, and head circumference may be available. Full-term newborns with appropriate growth parameters have the best chance for normal growth and development in the future. Low birth weight is more difficult to assess as it may be caused by prematurity or other prenatal factors such as malnutrition, infection and maternal smoking and drug/alcohol use. While infants well cared for in foster homes who receive good nutrition usually thrive, generalized failure to thrive is inevitable in institutionalized children during infancy. Children fall behind one month of linear growth for every three months in institutional care irrespective of duration. The head circumference is the most important measurement to follow in the pre-adoption evaluation. This measurement is the most accurate reflection of brain growth during the first years of life. Long-term studies show that children who have suffered severe malnutrition during their first year have a higher incidence of future learning disabilities. Sometimes parents receive inaccurate measurements, especially head circumference. It is easy to under-measure a head circumference if the tape measure does not encircle the head across the forehead to the widest point of the occiput. If there is a concern about growth measurements, usually families can request another set. Families who make an initial trip to see the child before they make their final decision can also be taught to measure head circumference at the time of that visit.

Maternal alcohol use is very common in Eastern Europe. This has become a major health concern for children adopted from these countries. Health care providers are often asked to look for fetal alcohol syndrome in their evaluation of a given child. Sometimes classic facial features can be seen with a photo or videotape. However, the facial features caused by maternal alcohol use during pregnancy are only evident in a certain percentage of those affected. The disease is a spectrum disorder ranging from mild behavioral and or learning disabilities with normal faces and growth to prevalence of facial features of fetal alcohol syndrome along with growth failure, microcephaly, and cognitive and behavioral issues. Criteria for the diagnosis have been established by the University of Washington and the Centers for Disease Control [and Prevention].

Adopting Older Children

Adopting an older child and/or sibling group can be a challenge to families. Emotional issues can be significant due to the child's past history. Children who have been abandoned may come with only an estimated age. Physical neglect and abuse is not uncommon. The effects of chronic malnutrition and/or maltreatment put the child at risk for future intellectual development and behavioral disorders.

In counseling families during the pre-adoption process, it is important to help families understand the health risks of a referred child. When it appears that the child may have major long-term medical issues, the family needs to have as much knowledge beforehand as possible about the condition and what care the child will need. It is very difficult for families to turn down a referral, and physicians need to be sensitive to this issue. Helping the family understand their own capabilities and resources in a nonjudgmental way will help make their decision easier and will facilitate the best match between a family and child. At the University of Minnesota International Adoption Clinic, after reviewing thousands of referrals, it is very apparent that families who make an informed decision and are prepared beforehand do better once the child arrives and feel more positive about the adoption. There are resources available to help prepare families. While agencies vary in what they provide to families regarding preparation, many will suggest that a family discuss their referral with a physician/health provider before accepting a child. While the turnaround time may be very short, for children with identified special needs families may be given extra time to make a decision. Additional health information can sometimes be requested. The International Adoption Clinic was started in 1986 as the first clinic to help counsel parents and prepare for the specific health needs of internationally adopted children. Since that time, more than fifty clinics are now located in the United States where families can have a pre-adoption consultation done by a medical expert in the field. Due to the high-risk status of children adopted from institutions, it is sometimes helpful to consult with a clinic specializing in international adoption.

The Post-Adoption Evaluation: Medical, Growth, and Developmental Issues

Once a child arrives home, he/she should have a comprehensive health evaluation to look at his medical, growth, and developmental status. First of all, the health care provider needs to evaluate the child's medical status, which includes the medical history, physical examination and specific laboratory screening tests. As was mentioned before, the medical history is not always very helpful due to incomplete and/or inaccurate information; however, significant medical diagnoses made in the child's country of origin need to be evaluated. If there is written documentation for immunizations given before the adoption, a decision should be made on whether to accept the vaccines as given or repeat them. While BCG [Bacillus Calmette-Guérin], diphtheria and tetanus toxoids and pertussis, poliovirus, measles, and hepatitis B are often documented, it is less common to find evidence of *Haemophilus influenzae* type B, varicella, mumps, rubella, and *Streptococcus pneumoniae*. Written documentation of vaccines alone should not be the criteria for acceptance of the vaccine as given appropriately. There is always the question of vaccine potency, storage and handling, age when given and reliability of accurate records. The [American] Academy of Pediatrics suggests two alternatives to this problem. Either serologic testing may be done to determine whether protective antibody levels are present or the child may be re-immunized. Almost always the child will need some vaccines after arrival to meet the recommendations set forth by the Academy of Pediatrics. Guidelines regarding immunizations can be found in the *Red Book: Report of the Committee on Infectious Diseases* by the American Academy of Pediatrics.

The physical examination of a newly arrived child can be helpful to identify some specific diagnoses but will miss major medical issues which may not be apparent on examination. Cutaneous infections are quite common and are found worldwide; scabies is prevalent among the children seen in our clinic. They can be intensely pruritic and stubborn to treat. Because the incubation period can be up to 6–8 weeks, the diagnosis can be missed if the child develops the lesions after he arrives in his new home. Scabies can also be confused with impetigo and eczema due to the itching and secondary skin infections that may develop. Evidence of rickets and bony abnormalities may also be seen on the initial medical evaluation. Evidence of past physical and or sexual abuse should always be considered, especially when an older child is extremely frightened during the exam. An interpreter, if available, can be especially helpful for older children who do not speak English. Sometimes there is evidence of past abuse from scars. Some children have been tied into their cribs in institutions to prevent them from falling and ligature scars encircling their ankles are seen. If there is concern about past injuries or fractures, X-rays may be appropriate to document past abuse.

Laboratory Screening Tests Are Vital

Laboratory screening tests are a crucial part of the initial medical evaluation. The health care provider needs to ensure that the child is free of diseases that could have an adverse af-

Pediatrics and International Adoption

International adoption is a new specialty area for pediatrics. In the 1980s, there were only 3 clinics in the United States that dealt with international adoption; now there are more than 25. The number of adoptions has really risen dramatically, especially in the past decade. "We're seeing over 20,000 every year, versus about 5,000 in 1992," said Dr. [Donna] Staton, chair of the Section on International Child Health at the American Academy of Pediatrics.

Damian McNamara,
"Over 20,000 International Adoptions Annually Spawn
New Specialty Area," Pediatric News, *August 2003.*

fect on long-term health and evaluate medical conditions previously known to be present so that appropriate treatment can be provided. Although some children have had some laboratory tests done in their country of origin, certain tests need to be repeated once the child is home. Testing in the country of origin is not reliable even if there is good documentation. There is always the concern that the test may not have been performed accurately or at the appropriate time. The following screening tests for infectious diseases in international adoptees have been recommended by the American Academy of Pediatrics. They include:

- Hepatitis B virus serologic testing

- Hepatitis B surface antigen (HBSAg)

- Hepatitis B surface antibody (HBSAB)

- Hepatitis B core antibody (HBCAB)

- Hepatitis C virus serologic testing

- Syphilis serologic testing

- Nontreponemal test (RPR, VDRL),(ART)

- Treponemal test (MHA-TP, FTA-ABS)

- HIV 1 and 2 serologic testing

- Complete blood cell count with red blood cell indices

- Stool examination for ova and parasites (3 specimens)

- Stool examination for *Giardia lamblia* and *Cryptosporidium* antigen

- Tuberculin skin test (PPD)

In addition we would add a TSH [thyroid-stimulation hormone test] because of possible iodine deficiency and a lead level. Due to possible exposure right before departure from the country of origin or poor nutrition, it is recommended that the Hepatitis B, Hepatitis C, HIV 1 and 2, and a PPD skin test be repeated six months after arrival.

There is sometimes confusion on the need to place a tuberculin skin test if the child has had a history of BCG vaccine. Having received Bacillus Calmette-Guérin (BCG) is not an indication for not placing a PPD, and a positive PPD should not be attributed to BCG. In these children, further exploration is necessary to see if tuberculosis is present. The only time that we postpone placement of the PPD in our clinic is when there is evidence of a freshly placed BCG where there is a scabbed or open lesion.

Other Areas of Evaluation

Vision and hearing evaluation is essential for newly arrived internationally adopted children. A recent study of children evaluated in our International Adoption Clinic during 2002 revealed a high incidence of both vision and hearing loss. All children were referred to an audiologist and ophthalmologist for evaluation. Thirteen percent of those evaluated had hearing loss and twenty-seven percent had vision problems.

The growth of a newly adopted child is the next area of evaluation. Specific factors affecting growth include malnutrition, genetic factors, and prenatal health of the mother. Institutionalization negatively impacts normal growth. Children may experience psychosocial dwarfism, falling behind in their linear growth on the average of one month for every three months they have spent in the institution. Growth parameters including height, weight, and head circumference need to be monitored closely. After placement in adoptive families, most children experience rapid catch-up growth. However, if the child does not show signs of catch-up growth during the first six months after arrival, further investigation is warranted. Chronic, metabolic and genetic diseases may be the cause as well as fetal alcohol spectrum disorders.

A developmental examination should be included as part of the initial evaluation a child receives soon after arrival home. Numerous factors affect development including the child's genetic background, care situation before adoption, medical and nutritional status. Delays are expected among children arriving from institutions. Often cultural practices regarding infant care affect development. Chinese children are discouraged from putting their hands into their mouths. In some countries, children are not allowed to crawl and explore on their own for safety reasons. Therefore soon after arrival is not the time to do standardized developmental and cognitive testing. The child needs time to adapt to his new family and environment before interventions occur.

Evaluations Are Important

Initial developmental screening is the time to identify those factors that will influence the child's long-term development. If there are nutritional or medical issues that need to be addressed, these may impact the child's strength and endurance. Vision and hearing abnormalities may certainly influence speech development, balance, fine and gross motor development. Therefore a joint neurodevelopmental and medical assessment is the most helpful initially. If there are neurological findings such as abnormal muscle tone, then the child may require more extensive evaluation soon. Otherwise it is better to reassess the child after he/she has transitioned to the new home.

Providing health care for internationally adopted children can be extremely rewarding and challenging to health care professionals. The children are delightful, and we have found from experience that the parents become strong advocates for their care. These children do have special needs, however, due to their past environment and other risk factors. While most of the children do extremely well in their new homes, a small percentage do have ongoing health and behavioral issues and will need comprehensive care to achieve optimal physical health, growth and development.

Periodical Bibliography

The following articles have been selected to supplement the diverse views presented in this chapter.

Nina Burleigh   "A Dad's Adoption Nightmare," *People*, vol. 71, no. 24, June 22, 2009.

Dan Frosch   "International Adoption Agencies in U.S. Collapsing," *Houston Chronicle*, May 12, 2008.

Jeff Gammage   "Rules Are Changing, Programs Are Closing," *Philadelphia Inquirer*, March 1, 2009.

E.J. Graff   "The Orphan Trade," *Slate*, May 8, 2009. www.slate.com.

David Itzkoff   "Ukraine Will Not Allow Adoption Proposed by Elton John," Arts Beat Blog, September 14, 2009. http://artsbeat.blogs.nytimes.com.

Mac Margolis   "Who Will Fill the Empty Cribs?" *Newsweek*, February 4, 2008.

Laura Ashley Martin   "'The Universal Language Is Not Violence. It's Love': The Pavlis Murder and Why Russia Changed the Russian Family Code and Policy on Foreign Adoptions," *Penn State International Law Review*, Winter 2008.

Annette Schmit   "The Hague Convention: The Problems with Accession and Implementation," *Indiana Journal of Legal Studies*, vol. 15, no. 1, Winter 2008.

Lynn D. Wardle   "The Hague Convention on Intercountry Adoption and American Implementing Law," *Indiana International & Comparative Law Review*, vol. 18, no. 1, Spring 2008.

Kayla Webley   "Why Americans Are Adopting Fewer Kids from China," *Time*, April 28, 2009.

For Further Discussion

Chapter 1

1. In her viewpoint, Elizabeth Bartholet argues that international adoption should be encouraged. E.J. Graff counters Bartholet's argument. Do you agree with Bartholet or Graff on this topic? Use points from both viewpoints to make your case.

2. Adopting children from countries ravaged by conflict or natural disasters is a controversial topic in light of the Haiti earthquake orphans. Read the viewpoints of the Evan B. Donaldson Adoption Institute and Asha Krishnakumar. In times of crisis, how should orphans be treated? What safeguards need to be in place to protect orphans?

Chapter 2

1. Discussions of celebrity adoptions often involve questions of whether they are in the best interests of the child. After reading viewpoints written by Cindy Rodriguez and Kate Sheehy, determine how celebrity adoptions can be detrimental or beneficial for the child.

2. Critics of celebrity adoptions often charge that they are a form of colonialism and skirt the line of child trafficking. Read the viewpoints from Carol Lloyd and Adam Elkus to inform your own views on the subject. In your opinion, is comparing celebrity adoptions to child trafficking and colonialism fair? If so, how?

Chapter 3

1. What are some of the beneficial and detrimental consequences of international adoption? Read through the viewpoints in this chapter and find the one you think

provides the best argument in favor of international adoption and the best argument against international adoption.

2. One of the major debates regarding international adoption is whether the discrimination that an adopted child may feel is a huge strike against the entire process. After reading viewpoints written by Angela Krueger and Mateo Cruz, what is your opinion on the matter? How do you think society is changing on this topic?

3. Jocelyn Noveck makes the case that international adoptions lead to American foster children being neglected. Many people believe that needy American children are waiting for adoption. After reading Noveck's views, do you believe that international adoptions are hurting American domestic adoptions?

Chapter 4

1. In his viewpoint, John Stossel claims that the international adoption process has too many regulations. Natalie Cherot argues that more regulations are necessary to ensure the protection of children and adoptive parents. After reading both views, which argument do you think has more merit? Be prepared to support your opinion.

2. How should the United States deal with countries that exploit children and manipulate the international adoption process? In her viewpoint, Kate O'Keefe asserts that the United States should cut off dealings with them. Do you agree? How do you think the United States should deal with such countries?

3. How can international adoptions be protected from politics? After reading Fred Weir's viewpoint on the topic, what is your opinion of the influence of political matters on the practice of international adoption?

Organizations to Contact

The editors have compiled the following list of organizations concerned with the issues debated in this book. The descriptions are derived from materials provided by the organizations. All have publications or information available for interested readers. The list was compiled on the date of publication of the present volume; the information provided here may change. Be aware that many organizations take several weeks or longer to respond to inquiries, so allow as much time as possible.

Centers for Disease Control and Prevention (CDC)
1600 Clifton Road, Atlanta, GA   30333
(800) CDC-INFO
e-mail: cdcinfo@cdc.gov
Web site: www.cdc.gov

The Centers for Disease Control and Prevention (CDC), a federal agency that operates as part of the Department of Health and Human Services, was established to protect public health and safety. In regard to international adoption, it publishes a traveler's health Web site, which provides much-needed information for prospective adoptive parents who plan to travel abroad to adopt a baby. It also has myriad informational materials on international adoption, including what health issues adoptive parents should be aware of in certain countries and what potential problems they may encounter with their baby's health. The CDC links to a number of resources for adoptive parents that aim to provide the best and most recent information on relevant issues regarding international adoption.

Congressional Coalition on Adoption Institute (CCAI)
311 Massachusetts Avenue NE, Washington, DC   20002
(202) 544-8500 • fax: (202) 544-8501

e-mail: info@ccainstitute.org
Web site: www.ccainstitute.org

The Congressional Coalition on Adoption Institute (CCAI) is "a nonprofit, nonpartisan organization dedicated to raising awareness about the millions of children around the world in need of permanent, safe, and loving homes and to eliminating the barriers that hinder these children from realizing their basic right of a family." The CCAI aims to accomplish three main tasks: educate politicians and policy makers about the challenges families face in the international adoption process; facilitate cooperation between lawmakers and adoptive families; and raise awareness of the need for and opportunities of domestic and international adoption. It also sponsors the Angels in Adoption program and the Congressional Resource Program, which publishes newsletters, legislative background reports, briefings, and statistical studies that disseminate the need for effective international and domestic adoption policies.

Evan B. Donaldson Adoption Institute

120 East Thirty-Eighth Street, New York, NY   10016
(212) 925-4089 • fax: (775) 796-6592
e-mail: info@adoptioninstitute.org
Web site: www.adoptioninstitute.org

Established in 1986, the Evan B. Donaldson Adoption Institute is a nonprofit organization that works to improve both domestic and international adoption policy, law, and practice through advocacy, research, and educational services. It disseminates information about adoption to the media, policy makers, and politicians in an effort to facilitate reasoned and educated decisions about adoption practices. Its ultimate mission is to reduce the barriers that stand in the way of adoptive families while promoting ethical standards for adoption professionals in the United States and countries all over the world. The institute publishes a number of research papers, statistical surveys, and in-depth reports on adoption issues, all of which are found on its Web site. Some of its recent publications include *Safeguarding the Rights and Well-Being of Birth Parents in the Adoption Process, Finding Families for African American Children*, and *Intercountry Adoption in Emergencies*. The institute also offers a monthly e-newsletter that provides progress reports on institute activities, programs, and policy initiatives.

Joint Council on International Children's Services (JCICS)

117 South Saint Asaph Street, Alexandria, VA 22314
(703) 535-8045 • fax: (703) 535-8049
e-mail: jcics@jcics.org
Web site: www.jcics.org

The Joint Council on International Children's Services (JCICS) is an advocacy organization that works to provide adoption services for children worldwide. Members include child advocacy organizations, orphan care organizations, adoption service providers, parent support groups, medical clinics, and professional service providers. The JCICS coordinates with state and local governments to provide ethical and beneficial adoption services and develop legislation to protect children. It also offers a tool kit to become involved in the international adoption movement, hosts a blog that focuses on adoption issues, and hosts seminars and conferences to allow organizations, individuals, and government officials the chance to network and exchange relevant information.

National Council for Adoption (NCFA)

225 North Washington Street, Alexandria, VA 22314-2561
(703) 299-6633 • fax: (703) 299-6004
e-mail: ncfa@adoptioncouncil.org
Web site: www.adoptioncouncil.org

The National Council for Adoption (NCFA) was founded in 1980 to encourage the practice of adoption in the United States. The NCFA lobbies for laws at the state level that facilitate the process of adoption; inform legislators and government departments on adoption practices and suggests sound adoption policy; and offers research on the advantages and challenges of adoption. In addition, the NCFA works with the

United States and foreign governments to establish sound policies for intercountry adoption, helping to place children all over the world in loving, permanent families. It publishes the *Adoption Factbook*, a compendium of facts and research on adoptions, as well as a quarterly newsletter, the *National Adoption Report*.

Office of Children's Issues, U.S. Department of State
Bureau of Consular Affairs, SA-29, 2201 C Street NW
Washington, DC   20520
(888) 407-4747 • fax: (202) 736-9080
e-mail: AskCI@state.gov
Web site: http://adoption.state.gov

The Office of Children's Issues, part of the Bureau of Consular Affairs at the U.S. Department of State, assists prospective adoptive parents in the adoption process by offering up-to-date information on specific countries and their adoption policies; works with foreign governments, embassies, and adoption agencies to expedite intercountry adoptions in the best interests of both the parent and child; and monitors the actions of accredited adoption agencies. Another central role of the Office of Children's Issues is to make sure that all interested parties uphold the principles of the Hague Convention on Intercountry Adoption (the Convention on Protection of Children and Co-operation in Respect of Intercountry Adoption). On its Web site, the Office of Children's Issues publishes Adoption Alerts to disseminate breaking information and changes to adoption policy, and it provides guidelines on how to apply for visas and other paperwork needed for international adoption.

Orphans International Worldwide (OIWW)
540 Main Street, Suite 418, New York, NY   10044
(212) 755-7302
e-mail: info@oiww.org
Web site: www.oiww.org

Orphans International Worldwide (OIWW) provides aid and services to orphaned children all over the world. Associated with the United Nations Department of Public Information, the OIWW has developed the "Family Care" model, in which donors provide ongoing, monthly stipends for the financial, health, and educational support of impoverished families that have taken in tsunami and hurricane orphans. OIWW also offers after-school tutoring, enrichment programs, health check-ups, and foster child and adoption monitoring. The OIWW Web site links to recent articles on events and news regarding the organization, as well as a blog.

United Nations Children's Fund (UNICEF)
125 Maiden Lane, 11th Floor, New York, NY   10038
(212) 686-5522 • fax: (212) 779-1679
Web site: www.unicefusa.org

Established in 1946 by the United Nations General Assembly, the United Nations Children's Fund (UNICEF) was created to provide emergency food supplies and health care to children residing in countries that had been devastated by the fighting of World War II. Once its original mission was complete, UNICEF was made a permanent part of the United Nations and was designated the responsibility of providing long-term humanitarian assistance for children in need all over the world. A few of UNICEF's focus areas include empowering women; child protection; HIV protection for young people; and basic educational services for children. UNICEF has been very active in the area of international adoptions, supporting the Hague Convention on Intercountry Adoption (the Convention on Protection of Children and Co-operation in Respect of Intercountry Adoption) and offering position papers and research on adoption, orphans, and children in need worldwide.

U.S. Citizenship and Immigration Services (USCIS)
(800) 375-5283
Web site: www.uscis.gov

U.S. Citizenship and Immigration Services (USCIS) is a government bureaucracy that provides immigration information for prospective parents to expedite the intercountry adoption process. It also determines the immigration status for the children ready to be adopted by an American family. The USCIS offers recent information on immigration procedures that affect individuals and provides updated information on new agreements between the United States and individual countries that impact the intercountry adoption process. Another area where the USCIS offers valuable assistance is the adoption-based forms guide, which provides links to the necessary forms all prospective parents will need for intercountry adoptions.

Worldwide Orphans Foundation (WWO)

511 Valley Street, Suite 200, Maplewood, NJ 07040
(973) 763-9961 • fax: (973) 763-8640
e-mail: info@wwo.org
Web site: www.wwo.org

Worldwide Orphans Foundation (WWO) is an international organization that works to improve the lives of orphans "by taking them out of anonymity and helping them to become healthy, independent, productive members of their communities and the world." WWO addresses the needs of orphaned children by providing medical, educational, development, and psychosocial programs mindful of the surrounding cultural milieu. WWO also coordinates with other organizations as well as local and national governments to ensure that orphaned children all over the world have opportunities to live healthy and fulfilled lives and gain the tools they need to succeed in adulthood. On the WWO Web site, the organization has published fact sheets, trip journals, personal stories, press releases, and a comprehensive archive of WWO stories.

Bibliography of Books

Christine Adamec and Laurie C. Miller — *The Encyclopedia of Adoption*. 3rd ed. New York: Facts on File, 2007.

Deborah Amend — *A Dress for Anna: The Story of the Redemption of the Life of a Ukrainian Orphan*. Lima, OH: CSS Pub., 2009.

Barbara Taylor Blomquist — *Insight into Adoption: Uncovering and Understanding the Heart of Adoption*. Springfield, IL: Charles C. Thomas, 2009.

Kevin and Johanna Carlisle — *In Search of a Family: A Story of International Adoption*. Ocala, FL: Atlantic Publication Group, 2009.

Laura Christianson — *The Adoption Decision*. Eugene, OR: Harvest House Publishers, 2007.

Dawn Davenport — *The Complete Book of International Adoption: A Step-by-Step Guide to Finding Your Child*. New York: Broadway Books, 2006.

Sara K. Dorow — *Transnational Adoption: A Cultural Economy of Race, Gender, and Kinship*. New York: New York University Press, 2006.

Sherrie Eldridge — *20 Things Adoptive Parents Need to Succeed*. New York: Delta Trade Paperbacks, 2009.

Elizabeth
Swire Falker
The Ultimate Insider's Guide to Adoption: Everything You Need to Know About Domestic and International Adoption. New York: Warner Wellness, 2006.

Christine
Ward Gailey
Blue-Ribbon Babies and Labors of Love: Race, Class, and Gender in U.S. Adoption Practice. Austin: University of Texas, 2010.

Michele
Bratcher
Goodwin
Baby Markets: Money and the New Politics of Creating Families. New York: Cambridge University Press, 2010.

Ray Guarendi
Adoption: Choosing It, Living It, Loving It. Cincinnati, OH: Servant Books, 2009.

Shannon Guymon
Child of Many Colors: Stories of Transracial Adoption. Springville, UT: CFI, 2010.

Sally Haslanger
and Charlotte
Witt, eds.
Adoption Matters: Philosophical and Feminist Essays. Ithaca, NY: Cornell University Press, 2005.

Timothy P.
Jackson, ed.
The Morality of Adoption: Social-Psychological, Theological, and Legal Perspectives. Grand Rapids, MI: W.B. Eerdmans, 2005.

Anne Lanchon
Adoption: How to Deal with the Questions of Your Past. New York: Amulet, 2006.

Susan C. Mapp   *Global Child Welfare and Well-Being.*
New York: Oxford University Press,
2010.

Diana Marre and   *International Adoption: Global*
Laura Briggs, eds. *Inequalities and the Circulation of*
Children. New York: New York
University Press, 2009.

Barbara A. Moe   *Adoption: A Reference Handbook.*
Santa Barbara, CA: ABC-CLIO, 2007.

Adam Pertman   *Adoption Nation: How the Adoption*
Revolution Is Transforming America.
New York: Basic Books, 2001.

Shirley Budd   *Adoption Reunion Stories.* Phoenix,
Pusey   AZ: Acacia Publishing, 2005.

Pamela Anne   *Adoption in a Color-Blind Society.*
Quiroz   Lanham, MD: Rowman & Littlefield,
2007.

Josephine A.   *Eastern European Adoption: Policies,*
Ruggiero   *Practice, and Strategies for Change.*
New Brunswick, NJ: Transaction
Publishers, 2007.

Dana Sachs   *The Life We Were Given: Operation*
Babylift, International Adoption, and
the Children of War in Vietnam.
Boston: Beacon Press, 2010.

Sarah L. Schuette *Adoptive Families.* Mankato, MN:
Capstone Press, 2010.

Brette McWhorter   *The Adoption Answer Book.*
Sember   Naperville, IL: Sphinx, 2007.

Brenda K. Uekert *10 Steps to a Successful International Adoption: A Guide Workbook for Prospective Parents.* Williamsburg, VA: Third Avenue Press, 2007.

Toby Alice Volkman, ed. *Cultures of Transnational Adoption.* Durham, NC: Duke University Press, 2005.

George Yancey and Richard Lewis Jr. *Interracial Families: Current Concepts and Controversies.* New York: Routledge, 2009.

Barbara Yngvesson *Belonging in an Adopted World: Race, Identity, and Transnational Adoption.* Chicago: University of Chicago Press, 2010.

Index